IN ART WE TRUST

The Board of Trustees in the Performing Arts

November 1981
Copyright © 1981
by the Foundation for the Extension
and Development of the American
Professional Theatre

ISBN No. 0-9602942-3-6

Cover design and illustrations: Carol Chebba

Table of Contents

Foreword

The relationship between The Ohio State University (OSU) and the Foundation for the Extension and Development of the American Professional Theatre (FEDAPT) began in February-March 1980 with the Ohio Dance Company Management Technical Assistance Program. FEDAPT chose Ohio as the site of its pilot Management Technical Assistance Program in dance, using six Ohio dance companies. The purpose of the program was to assist these dance companies in developing and strengthening the managerial capabilities of their respective institutions and to give the directors of FEDAPT a model on which to plan future technical assistance programs in dance. A series of four intensive weekend conferences was organized in which experts from dance, theatre, and related performing arts professions led the sessions, which were geared to improving the quality of the companies' management procedures.

Ohio State offered to host the program, and the four conferences were held at the University's continuing education conference facility, the Fawcett Center for Tomorrow. This invitation was extended for several reasons, including the College of the Arts' commitment to providing students opportunities to pursue studies in arts administration and management, the existence of a nationally known and active dance department within the College that was interested in being a part of this professional service-oriented project, and a knowledge of FEDAPT's expertise in conducting similar assistance programs in theatre. The response of the dance companies to FEDAPT's program and the continued consulting that has occurred between FEDAPT and those companies since the 1980 sessions has more than justified Ohio State's initial hospitality. The publication of *In Art We Trust: The Board of Trustees in the Performing Arts* is but another step in the developing OSU-FEDAPT relationship.

Andrew J. Broekema, Dean
College of the Arts
The Ohio State University
November 1981

Preface

Just as "overnight stardom" is achieved only after anywhere from ten to twenty years of training, experience, and development, a cohesive, dedicated, productive board of trustees does not emerge at the moment that each individual agrees to sit on a board.

FEDAPT is a Management Technical Assistance resource for professional theatre companies and dance companies and, as such, has offered some kind of extensive Management Technical Assistance to over 140 theatre companies and dance companies throughout the United States since I became its executive director in May of 1970. This firsthand experience of discussing the operational concerns of these companies has driven home more and more that until and unless there is better understanding of the mechanics of arts institutions' structures, the artists in this country will not have the opportunity to fulfill consistently their potential of creating artistic excellence.

While every not-for-profit tax-exempt organization has some board of trustees by virtue of state and federal laws, and almost every major profit-making corporation also has a board of directors or trustees, the nature and the role of a board remains a mystery to most people, especially those who find themselves at board meeting. My experience throughout the country with theatre companies and dance companies has led me to believe that while many boards are in need of guidance, there are no villains in board rooms. There are people with a sense of both community responsibility and a commitment to a particular art form who make assumptions rather than ask the right questions. I contend that the more imaginatively creative the artistic leadership of a performing arts institution, the more creative the management structure and board of trustees must be. Not only must the systems, structures, and processes of fiscal management, audience development, fund raising, and box office operation be exacting, responsible, and efficient but also handcrafted to meet the unique needs of the specific company for which they are designed. The same should hold true in the assembling, structuring, and development of a board of trustees.

Although FEDAPT has been offering extensive technical assistance to boards in the course of developing a strategic planning process and conducting board retreats for our project theatres and dance companies, a compilation of information was needed. FEDAPT's policy has been to utilize the working management professionals as consultants and to use the practical experiences of theatre and dance personnel as points of reference. We therefore invited nine individuals to address aspects of the subject at hand, whose collective personal experiences as board members and/or managers in the performing arts cover the spectrum of artist/manager/board relationships in theatre companies, dance companies, orchestras, and opera companies. The nine sections contributed by these individuals complement the material presented by Robert Crawford. Each of the issues addressed by this manual is identified and illuminated by offering these varying points of view.

This manual has been a long time in coming. The insights and conclusions presented herein were reached by living through and learning from a myriad of experiences with almost two hundred performing arts institutions.

This Board of Trustees Guidelines joins FEDAPT's other publications which as of this date include *Box Office Guidelines, Subscription Guidelines,* and *Investigation Guidelines for Developing and Operating a Not-For Profit Tax-Exempt Resident Theatre.* It is designed to convey information, to illustrate aspects of the subject, and to help, in general, to conserve a national resource – the artist. Mostly, however, it is designed to motivate dispassionate investigations, which will enable a board of trustees, in conjunction with management and artists, to design a uniquely configured board structure to serve its unique artistic leadership.

This manual is designed to be read by present, past, and future board members, as well as present, past, and future management personnel. It is hoped that the manual will be used by artists who are interested in developing or preserving a performing arts institution. It is hoped, also, that college and university students in graduate and undergraduate programs will make use of it. They are the corporate and community leaders of the future, and, as potential members of arts boards, should be better prepared than the previous generations.

FEDAPT is indebted to The Ohio State University for publishing this work; to the incredibly skilled and dedicated arts professionals who contributed directly and indirectly; to the dedicated and tireless board members of the many arts institutions with which FEDAPT has worked; and especially, to Robert W. Crawford, who has spent much of his adult life in the board rooms of so many arts institutions. By virtue of his insight, tenacity, and wit, his "compiling, editing, and writing" this manual will enable all of us to focus in on this phenomenon called a board of trustees.

This project would not have come to fruition had it not been for FEDAPT's entire staff who researched, edited, typed, argued, and suffered through its conception, gestation, and birth. Specifically, FEDAPT is beholden to Jessica L. Andrews, Alice Chebba, Bruce A. Hoover, Joseph V. Melillo, and Judith A. Morgan. FEDAPTA is further indebted to the theatre and dance management professionals who while serving as our consultants over the years have contributed immeasurably to the information, understanding, and, I hope, the wisdom contained herein.

Frederic B. Vogel
Executive Director, FEDAPT   June 11, 1981

Biographical Note on Robert W. Crawford

Following completion of his undergraduate studies in International Relations at Yale University and receiving his master's and doctoral degrees in Islamic History from Princeton University, Mr. Crawford's career has been largely connected with both the Middle East and with the arts in this country. He has served as a member of a number of not-for-profit boards of trustees including those of the Guthrie Theater, the Minnesota Opera, the Children's Theatre Company and School, and the Twin Cities Metropolitan Arts Alliance. For six years he was Chairman of the Theatre Advisory Panel of the National Endowment for the Arts, a federal agency in Washington, D.C. Mr. Crawford served four years in Morocco with the U.S. Information Service and five years as Vice President of the American University of Beirut.

He served as an officer of the Rockefeller Foundation from 1961-1967 with responsibilities in the humanities, social sciences, and the arts. During his tenure, the Rockefeller Foundation maintained an imaginative and creative support program for the arts nationally. From 1972-1976 he was President of the Spring Hill Conference Center in Minnesota.

Since 1976, Mr. Crawford has worked as a consultant to a wide variety of performing and visual arts institutions, assisting them with board development, institutional planning, and in the area of general management, with particular emphasis on board/staff relationships. For FEDAPT his skills have been utilized to aid in the development of theatre and dance companies throughout the country. In addition, he has been a consultant to three foundations.

Throughout his professional life, he has either worked for boards of trustees in the not-for-profit area or served as a board member. Further, he has participated in the raising of substantial funds as well as having participated in the granting of funds from both the public and private sectors. This manual has been written out of the knowledge, perceptions, and conclusions garnered from these practical experiences.

Introduction

Need for this Manual   Little exists in print that considers in a constructive way the obligations and opportunities for members of boards of trustees. Most of what is written is directed primarily toward the legal ramifications and responsibilities of trusteeship – thus, the need for a publication including suggestions or guidelines for the establishment of boards, for the strengthening of boards, and for the development of more effective working boards. The need is for guidelines based on reality gained through experience, not on theory. The demand for such guidelines comes from current board members as well as from the management and artistic staffs of professional not-for-profit performing arts organizations.

As a result of this need, this trusteeship guidelines manual has been prepared. It is a manual of guidelines. It is not a manual of absolute answers. *There is no one correct set of answers covering trusteeship which is, or which can be, applicable to all institutions.* The staff and board of each institution must choose that which is correct for it at its present moment in institutional history and for the projected years ahead. It should not be assumed that what is correct or appropriate for one institution is equally so for another. There are certain commonalities among all not-for-profit institutions, but all not-for-profit institutions are not similar in purpose, in form, in need, in experience, or in institutional development. It is essential, therefore, that this manual be used judiciously. It will not provide all the specific answers a particular institution might be seeking, but it can serve as a valuable, responsible resource for board members and staffs as they search for better ways to structure their boards for more effective service to the art form served by the institution.

Types of Institutions Covered   This manual includes information based on and directed toward all not-for-profit professional performing arts institutions: theatre, dance, opera, music, and performing arts centers. It recognizes that there are definite differences in specific structures among and between some of these art forms but reflects the conviction that all have many common or similar structural identities, insofar as board/staff responsibilities and relationships are concerned. This manual is directed toward those organizations that already are institutions or that are moving toward becoming institutions – those organizations that look toward or aspire to a continuing existence.

This manual is directed toward professional artistic directors, professional management, current board members, as well as toward the lay community that may or may not ever serve as members of boards of trustees. If artistic directors, managing directors, and board members know what type of institution theirs is and what its purpose is, they will then be able to glean information from this manual more effectively – information that can be of help in further organizational development.

In addition to identifying institutions by artistic form or type (theatre, dance, opera, music), *each artistic director, managing director, and trustee should know clearly what type the institution is in terms of preeminence in leadership.* Broadly speaking, there are three basic types: artistic director-founded institutions, managing director-founded institutions, and trustee founded-institutions. There is no right or wrong, better or worse, in regard to these definitions. All participants on the institutional team, however, should be aware of what kind of institution he or she is part of, how it started, and where the focus of leadership is at present.

An artistic director's institution is one that has emanated and emerged out of the artistic impulse and energy of a particular artist. It is he or she who created the institution, based on a particular artistic vision, energy, and need. Although he or she may have attracted a strong managing director to the staff and may have developed a strong board over the years, when the chips are down, the final decisions actually remain in the artistic director's hands. In a very real sense, the artist has hired, not only the managing director, but also the board.

A managing director's institution is one that has emerged out of a manager's determination and dedication to create an artistic institution. The manager has searched out an artistic leader with whom he or she can work effectively. In this type of institution, it is usually the managing director who has recruited the board. When the chips are down, it is the managing director who is preeminent among equals.

The trustee's institution is one that essentially has been decreed into existence by a group of lay persons who have determined and decided that the community needs a particular type of arts institution. They search for and hire an artistic director and a managing director (or in reverse order) and are not only preeminent among equals by law, but also in a de facto sense.

It is natural and normal that institutions and people change over the years. It is vital, however, that all participants on the institutional team (artists, management, and trustees) understand from whence the institutional impetus and impulse came, and how, in fact, it has evolved. In this way, there can be a better and conscious understanding of where it should evolve further. Such understanding can help clarify relationships among the total team, rather than depending essentially upon perhaps out-of-context job descriptions and authority flow charts. Again, there is no right or wrong model. What is right structurally and what is wrong structurally depends on what an institution really is and where it wants to go, rather than on someone's perception of what it should be in order to conform to some predetermined, prescribed model.

Of further importance to making effective use of this manual is a clear understanding of what the purpose of the institution is. Some sort of statement of purpose normally is enunciated in the original articles of incorporation or charter. Such statements of purpose frequently are so general that they encompass most any sort of activity related to the particular art form. In order to operate effectively, however, it is important that the members of the board, as well as the artistic and management leadership, have a more defined statement of purpose upon which to base their activities. *Any activity undertaken by an institution is justified only if it serves one or more of the purposes of that institution at any given moment in its history.* Purposes may and often do change over time, but such changes should be made consciously, not as is so often the case, on an ad hoc basis. When all members of the institutional team – artists, management, and board—agree on purpose, decisions on program implementation and support are made more rationally. When purpose is understood clearly, structures and interrelationships can be developed to serve or implement those purposes, not as ends in and of themselves based on some theoretical model. *The use of people and money are justified only in terms of implementing programs that in turn implement or serve the basic purpose or purposes of the institution.*

Scope of the Manual This manual concentrates on the following areas or topics. First, is a chapter on "Why a Board of Trustees," a discussion of a board's purpose from both legal and conceptual points of view. Second, is a chapter on the "Functions of a Board of Trustees." This section includes a discussion of institutional responsibility and authority as well as the delegation of such responsibility to staff and to board committees. Different points of view are presented in regard to what a "working" board is. A third chapter deals with "Structuring a Board," including the following: size; criteria for board membership; types of board expertise; use of board members as quasi-staff; recruitment of board members; election of board members; board orientation; length of service for board members; board officers and their length of service; board committees and membership on committees; advisory, honorary, or emeritus groups; a discussion of quorums and proxies; and board meetings. A fourth chapter deals with the types of things that might be accomplished in "Board Retreats." Finally, a fifth chapter presents a set of basic "Sample By-Laws."

Through a careful study of the information included in this manual, it is hoped the reader will be better able to select judiciously what is most applicable to his or her specific situation and to modify what is appropriate to modify. Further, it is hoped the reader will come to understand that: 1. there is no mystery or magic in trusteeship; 2. that trustees are not some hallowed group above the rest; 3. that trustees are an integral part of a three-facet team comprised of artists, management, and board working together to assure the best possible professional implementation, with integrity, of the art form of which they all are a part.

Chapter 1

Why a Board of Trustees

Historically, the purpose of the creation and existence of boards of trustees has been to satisfy federal and state legal requirements necessary to the attainment of not-for-profit tax-exempt status. Without such status, an institution cannot provide the private sector donor (individual or corporate entity) with a receipt valid for tax deduction purposes. Nor can an institution be eligible to receive grant support from private foundations or public sector grant making entities, e.g., federal, state, county, and city governments. In order to effectively obtain contributed income from any or all of the above sources, an institution must be governed by a board of trustees as prescribed by the various not-for-profit corporation codes enacted by state legislatures and recognized by the Internal Revenue Service.

The following was prepared by a New York theatrical attorney who has assisted in the establishment of many not-for-profit arts institutions.

THE NOT-FOR-PROFIT CORPORATION BOARD OF TRUSTEES
by Donald C. Farber

Almost without exception the clients who come to me to organize a not-for-profit theatrical producing company would, if they had their choice, opt for the following: a not-for-profit corporation that would engage the client as artistic director to produce and direct anything and everything he or she wishes. Ideally, the board of trustees would be composed of all rich patrons who would know more rich patrons who would fund the corporation with more than enough money to produce each season's program. Of course, the board of trustees, although they would have the authority, would never interfere with any of the work of the artistic director. The members of the corporation would always elect a board of trustees sympathetic to the artistic director and also would never interfere in the theatre program. When one awakens from the dream, one discovers that this ideal is rarely attainable.

The composition of a board of trustees of a not-for-profit corporation should be carefully planned to satisfy two very different criteria. First, the legal requirements for the board must be satisfied and, second, the needs of the organization should be catered to.

Every state in the Union has its own specific legal requirements concerning not-for-profit corporations. The minimum number of board members may vary and the number of board members that constitute a quorum may also vary. In the State of New York, for example, there must be at least three (3) trustees and each must be at least 19 years of age. Three board members may not give you enough workers, and seventy-five board members may make the job of accomplishing anything impossible. The board of trustees elects or appoints the officers; however, there are provisions that members may elect the officers rather than the board.

The Not-For-Profit Corporation Law of the State of New York also has very specific provisions concerning the purpose, the powers, the names (certain words are forbidden as part of the name, and the name must include "Corporation, Incorporated, or Limited" or an abbreviation of one of the three), the method of incorporating (one person at least 19 years old may incorporate and a judge must approve of the incorporation), the stocks or shares, members, directors, etc.

Whatever the legal requirements are in each state, they are fixed, easily accessible, and understandable, and all one need do is read the applicable law and comply with the requirements.

Within the framework of the actual legal requirements is the problem of creating a certificate of incorporation and appropriate by-laws that permit the organization to function in such a manner that it fulfills the needs of the organizers and of the organization. Every organization has different needs, although in my experience there is one need that almost every performing arts organization has in common. This of course is access to money. As has been indicated, the composition of the board can do much to make obtaining contributions and grants easier and to provide necessary financing.

There are other differences in the board, which will depend on the needs of the particular organization that are not defined by the requirements of law. As an example, a not-for-profit organization organized for the purpose of acquiring land, constructing a theatre, and using the premises for the purpose of presenting plays would be well advised to have one or more board members conversant with land values, building conditions, real estate tax exemptions, and other such matters. A not-for-profit corporation organized for the purpose of promoting new playwrights by furnishing them with working facilities and the opportunity to develop new plays would need a real estate expert on the board less, and could better use an artistic person experienced in the reading of scripts who could supervise the committee selecting the recipients of the grants from the corporation. A not-for-profit corporation organized for the purpose of promoting Black theatre would be wise to have some board members who have a conscious awareness of the Black theatre movement. Likewise, an avant garde theatre corporation should have board members who appreciate avant garde plays. A not-for-profit corporation whose purpose is to promote and produce musical revivals could well use some board members who care about musical theatre.

Satisfying the needs of the corporation can be accomplished with the proper board members functioning in accordance with a carefully drafted certificate of incorporation and by-laws that permit the organization to accomplish its objectives with a minimum of unnecessary procedural requirements. The controls necessary to prevent autonomous action by an artistic director should not be so drafted as to make any constructive action by the key personnel difficult, if not impossible.

The single most important task in organizing and maintaining a properly functioning not-for-profit corporation is the careful planning and selection of board members who have the knowledge, the time, and the motivation to fulfill the needs of the corporation. To accomplish this, one must first ascertain the corporation's needs and then pursue with dogged diligence and determination those persons who can and will meet those needs. Most often the board of trustees is selected at random or in a number of instances consists of people whose sole qualification is their availability and willingness to serve.

In Summary:

1. Satisfy the legal requirements for a board. This is easy.
2. Determine the needs of the organizations. This is harder.
3. Select board members who can answer the needs. This is difficult.
4. Pursue them and get them to serve on the board. This is very difficult but not impossible.

The time spent in getting the proper board can be considerable, but it is an extremely important thing to do and should be considered one of the most important jobs of organizing any not-for-profit corporation.

In order to acquire tax exempt status, that is, freedom from the payment of Federal income tax, there must be full compliance with the Federal laws and the Internal Revenue Code concerning such tax-exempt status. There is a form to complete, and a good deal of information that must be furnished to accomplish this objective. If the not-for-profit corporation owns real estate that is used for the not-for-profit purpose, in some states it is also possible to get a real estate tax exemption for the property.

Ideally, the board of trustees would also be rich patrons who would know more rich patrons who would fund the corporation . . . .

Donald C. Farber

Donald C. Farber is a practicing attorney in the entertainment industry representing theatrical productions, performers, directors, authors, repertory companies, and producers. He is the author of five books: *From Option to Opening; Producing on Broadway; Actor's Guide: What You Should Know About the Contracts You Sign; Producing, Financing, and Distributing Film; Producing Theatre: A Comprehensive Legal and Business Guide.* Mr. Farber has been a Visiting Professor and Guest Lecturer in the Arts Administration Program at York University (Toronto, Canada) and has lectured on legal aspects of the performing arts at Brooklyn College, New York University, and The New School for Social Research.

While many believe a board exists only to comply with legal requirements and to raise money, there is a growing body of thought that perceives the purpose of the board as much broader. In addition to satisfying the requirements of the law, *the basic purpose of a board is to participate in any and all appropriate ways, through whatever actions and activities are deemed necessary, to assure that the institution is moving effectively toward fulfilling its artistic purpose.* The board is an integral component of the total institutional team, all parts of which are dedicated to the same artistic purpose. The existence of a board is, therefore, not an end in and of itself.

If this broad basic purpose of the existence of a board is accepted, misunderstandings that may arise between some board members and the artistic and management staffs of some institutions can be precluded. Most important of these sometimes subtle undercurrents of misunderstanding is the question or concept of ownership. *The board of trustees of a not-for-profit professional performing arts organization does not own the institution. No single person or group owns such an institution.* With the rapid proliferation of not-for-profit arts institutions over the last twenty to twenty-five years, and the concurrent increased magnitude of fiscal responsibilities, it is not surprising that some confusion has resulted in regard to the purpose of boards of trustees. Particularly in the field of dance, and increasingly in theatre, opera, and music institutions, there has been an evolution of the perception that the institution is owned by the board.

In an effort to clarify the situation, in 1978 the legislature of the state of California enacted a new Nonprofit Corporation Law, amended in 1979. Under this law, the legislature divided the not-for-profit organizations into three main categories: public benefit corporations; mutual benefit corporations; and religious corporations. Not-for-profit professional performing arts institutions come under the heading of public benefit corporations. Under the California statute, public benefit corporations are: 1. formed for a public or charitable purpose and 2. not operated for the mutual benefit of their members, but for some broader good. Members of public benefit corporations (if there are members) have no meaningful ownership interest in the corporation and upon dissolution of the corporation, its assets must go to some other appropriate not-for-profit corporation or charitable organization. Most state laws regulating not-for-profit corporations include a similar proviso. The laws governing not-for-profit institutions vary from state to state, and each institution must be aware of its particular state laws. There is, however, no indication of ownership of a not-for-profit professional arts institution in any state law.

There are variant wordings on trustee responsibilities among the different state laws, but essentially, most statutes provide that the ultimate responsibility for (not ownership of) the institution lies in the hands of the board of trustees, while at the same time providing for the delegation of actual operating responsibilities to others in the institution. Such delegation of responsibility for implementation of actions does not take the ultimate responsibility away from the board. In most statutes, board members are expected to perform their duties: "with care, including reasonable inquiry, as an ordinarily prudent person would use under similar circumstances" (California); "in good faith and with that degree of diligence, care and skill which ordinarily prudent people would exercise under similar circumstances in like positions" (New York). *Boards of not-for-profit professional performing arts institutions have a fiduciary, a trusteeship, responsibility* in contrast to the responsibility of members of a board of directors for a for-profit corporation, the ownership of which lies in the hands of the stockholders. There is no ownership of a not-for-profit professional performing arts institution. *The institution is held by a board in trusteeship for the broader public good.*

Depending on what type of arts institution it serves, a board has, as another basic purpose, the making of and/or approving of policy. Usually, the board of an institution that has been created by an artistic director (be it a theatre, a dance company, an opera company, or a music group) did not, nor does not, establish the initial artistic policy, thrust, or impulse. Rather, it approves the overall policy as established by the artist. On the other hand, an institution that has been created by a group of individuals who are not professional artists and who may or may not become its actual trustees, usually has its basic policy created by that founding group, which then seeks an artistic leader to implement the policy. As performing arts institutions mature, and as a natural result of longevity, there is bound to be a change in artistic leadership. When such occurs, it becomes the responsibility of the board to identify and hire a new artistic leader. It is at this point that there often is a shift, conscious or unconscious, in the perception of the board's role in regard to artistic policy. It becomes one of making policy so that an effective search may be made for the successor to the incumbent artistic leader, rather than approving the policy of the existing artistic director. Most simply stated the making and/or approving of artistic policy is the making and/or approving of the artistic purpose of the institution. *The basic role of the board of trustees of a not-for-profit professional performing arts institution is to provide through its actions and its efforts the best possible total environment conducive to the fullest implementation of the artistic purpose of the institution, consistent with prudent and creative management.*

By statute in most states, members of boards of trustees may not be passive trustees. Were they to be passive, they would be in violation of the "prudent man" concept of responsibility. The delegation of certain authority or responsibility does not abrogate the board's ultimate authority and responsibility. If a board is not permitted by law to be passive, it must be active to at least a certain degree. A board member must be aware of all actions taken by the institution. *A trustee is perceived as approving actions unless he or she specifically states otherwise.* A vote by the majority of the board at a meeting where a quorum is present, is considered a vote by the board as a whole, unless a member requests his or her negative vote to be recorded in the minutes. Even if a board member is absent from a meeting at which an action is voted upon, he or she also is assumed to be in support of the action unless a formal negative is recorded when he or she learns of the vote.

But beyond the legal requirements for active participation in institutional affairs, increasing numbers of institutional staffs and boards believe that a vital part of the purpose of the board is that it be a working board. There are many different interpretations of what a working board should be. This topic will be discussed more fully in the following chapter. What is important to understand at this point is that boards of trustees of not-for-profit professional performing arts institutions may not be passive. They must be both proactive as well as actively reactive to what is presented to them.

Chapter 2

Functions of a Board of Trustees

In the preceding chapter, the reasons or purposes for the existence of boards of trustees were discussed. It was pointed out that ultimate responsibility for the institution remains with the board as a group. No individual board member has the right, power, or authority to take any action on behalf of the institution. Rather, the power is vested in the board as a whole. It was further explained that most state legislation governing not-for-profit corporations provides for the delegation of authority by boards to others: to the officers of the corporations, to staff of the institution, and to committees established by the board to fulfill certain functions. Nevertheless, the ultimate responsibility and the obligation to remain informed remains with the board.

In order for a board to fill its commitment as an integral part of the institutional team, it must take an active role. A board cannot be passive if the institution is to flourish. Board members must be prepared to react to what is presented to them by artistic and management staff, approving or disapproving recommendations brought to them for action through board votes. They also must work in an effective proactive way for the institution, assist in providing the means to implement programs, and share their particular expertise with others in the institution for the benefit of the whole.

Board members work in their trustee capacity as volunteers. In contrast to a member of the board of directors of a for-profit corporation, board members of not-for-profit professional performing arts institutions receive no pay or honoraria for their services. They are expected to provide time, energy, and money to the institution without any form of monetary or in-kind compensation. In order to work effectively as a trustee, the individual must receive some sort of compensatory satisfaction. The trustee must feel that his or her work and participation really makes some sort of difference, or it is not worth the volunteer's time and effort that could be expended elsewhere. *In order to work effectively, the trustee must understand the purpose or purposes of the institution and must be actively cognizant of the programs currently engaged in by the institution toward fulfillment of that purpose.* The trustee should know clearly why he or she has been asked to serve on the board and should know equally clearly, at least privately, why he or she accepted board membership. Where there is enough identity and mutuality of self-interests among an institution and its individual board members, there is the real possibility of a successful working relationship and potential for satisfying achievement.

Because most board members have full-time occupations or

obligations outside the institution of which they are trustees, or obligations as trustees of other not-for-profit institutions, each has a limited amount of time to be active as a working member of any given board. It is, therefore, logical to assume that all board members cannot and will not be able to participate as members of the full board in the same manner or degree of intensity. Hence the necessity for the delegation of some responsibility to others by the board, to provide effective use of both volunteer and staff time for the benefit of the institution. Some examples of tasks to be delegated are obvious, e.g., check signing, contracts with artists, union negotiations, selection of individual artistic works comprising the season, and purchases of material for sets and costumes. Other forms of delegation are often less clear, e.g., delegation of authority to an executive committee or other board committees that may be empowered to act on behalf of the board as a whole.

Committee structures will be discussed in the following chapter, but attention is accorded board committees at this point because of their very important role as points of focus for some delegation of responsibility by the whole board. There are two basic categories of committees that should be provided for in the by-laws of each not-for-profit professional performing arts institution: 1. standing committees and 2. ad hoc committees. *Standing committees are those that the institution feels are necessary for the continuing effective operation of the institution. Ad hoc committees are those created to deal with particular problems or opportunities over a specific, limited period of time.* When its purpose has been achieved, an ad hoc committee goes out of existence.

Not all institutions need all the same standing committees. A committee should be created only when there is perceived need for its services at the present time and over the forseeable future. There is almost nothing more disheartening to a member of a committee than to realize that there is not an important purpose for its existence and that time spent working on it – or just meeting – is, in reality, wasted time. There are, however, a number of standing committees that can help any institution in its development toward more effective stability and that can provide those board members who are members of them with the opportunity to serve the institution in a meaningful way. *Each institution should consider carefully, in terms of its own real needs, whether or not the following standing committees should be established: Nominating; Finance; Fund Raising; Planning; Executive.*

Nominating Committee   In many, if not most, institutions, the nominating committee usually meets sometime before the annual meeting of the board to decide on nominations for board memberships and nominations for the officer positions on the board. Discussions of the nominating committee usually are held from the perspective of "who knows whom" or who might be a likely candidate for the board. In such discussions, there frequently is the dreaming of getting someone who has money or who has access to money, with the assumption made that if such a person is attracted to the board, he or she will automatically contribute a substantial amount or be able to solicit a substantial amount through personal connections. There is normally a considerable degree of disappointment resulting from this type of board member recruitment, primarily because the person brought onto the board for this reason is not told up front that that is what is expected. It is assumed that everyone knows the reason, but it is not spelled out clearly in advance. Further, little if any consideration is given to the fact that most people with money who are likely to contribute, already have commitments to give to other institutions and are not able to phase in significantly for a period of time to a new institution. Also, those with access to money, whatever that really means, put out IOU's when they solicit another for a contribution. They ultimately must return the favor to the one solicited.

The mechanics of operating a nominating committee will be discussed in the following chapter. *This manual recommends the existence of a nominating committee as a standing committee, meeting regularly throughout the year, assessing the needs of the institution – specifically, how particular types of individuals can serve effectively and, through their particular expertise, provide resources to the board not currently present.* In this way, planned development and strengthening of a board can be an ongoing process.

As a standing committee, *the nominating committee also should review the service of all board members.* Assuming that all board members have been told clearly what the minimum expected participation is, the nominating committee should review such participation and recommend reelection to the board, if such is appropriate, or recommend that an individual not be reelected. *The key to the successful operation of a nominating committee is a clear understanding of the totality of the institution, its purpose and its programs, and how the institution can best be served by its trustees.* Based on full knowledge and understanding of the institution, individuals can be sought out as trustees who are really equipped to be of assistance and support. *In a very real sense, an institution deserves the board it has or gets. Membership on a board should never be viewed as an honor or as a recognition of other achievements.* Rather, it is a privilege and a serious commitment.

Finance Committee   *The Finance Committee of any not-for-profit professional performing arts institution has at least four vital purposes:* 1. to assist, as appropriate, in the preparation of the budget, including both the projected income and projected expense, and to present that budget to the full board for approval; 2. to monitor on a regular basis the activation or implementation of the budget in terms of both expense and income; 3. to recommend to the full board any budget revisions before – not after – the fact; and 4. to understand the difference of cash flow problems and real budget problems and to transmit the understanding and implications of these different problems to the full board, with recommendations for their accommodation.

Although the board has complete, ultimate responsibility for the fiscal well-being and efficient fiscal management of the institution, boards frequently delegate an inordinate amount of that responsibility to the finance committee. Finance committees, in turn, often delegate too much of their responsibility to the management staff of the institution. Horror stories abound among both large-budget and small-budget institutions in regard to financial management.

Financial management is not, nor should it ever be, an end in and of itself. *The budget of an institution is a set of guidelines for the use of dollar resources for the implementation of the artistic purposes of the institution.* No institution should begin its fiscal year without a board-approved budget for that year. Therefore, the budget preparation for any given fiscal year must start well before the beginning of the year. The artistic director determines, usually in concert with the managing director, what specific artistic activities or programs will be presented. Together, they cost out the overall program. Certain realities are faced by the two, priorities are established, and trade-offs made to arrive at what appears to be an attainable budget, both on the income and the expense side. All forms of earned income are carefully itemized and the resulting gap between total projected earned income and total operating expenses becomes the budgeted income gap. This is the gap – the dollar amount – that must be raised by the staff and the board through contributions and grants from the public and private sectors. This gap is the total amount of contributed income that must be found to balance the budget. *When a board finally approves any budget, it is approving not only the expense figures but also the projected earned and contributed income figures. It is committing itself as a body to the implementation of that budget unless and until subsequent budget revisions are made and approved.*

When the artistic and management staffs have completed their budget draft, it should be presented to the finance committee for thorough discussion. It is at that time that the members of the finance committee must exercise their responsibility to clearly understand the figures. They must ask questions if there are any questions in their minds. If, for example, based on the history of the institution, projected earned income figures appear high – or low – the finance committee must question their validity, and the staff must explain them to the satisfaction of the committee, or change them. This is not interference on the part of the board members in the management of the institution. Rather, it is common sense input into the budget process before faulty figures are locked in.

Wishful thinking about both earned and contributed income potentials have caused serious problems for many large and small budget institutions. Recently, through irresponsible wishful thinking, the staff of a large budget arts institution estimated its earned income through subscription and single ticket sales, one-third higher than could be reasonably expected based on previous years' experience. The finance committee, which had not met with the staff during the course of the budget preparation, met for only an hour to discuss the total complex budget. Few questions were asked and no one questioned the validity of the projected earned income figures. Immediately following the meeting of the finance committee, the budget was presented by the chairman of the committee to the full board, with recommendation for approval. Following perfunctory discussion, the budget was approved. This inept handling of the budget process resulted in a serious financial problem for the institution during the year, placing an unexpected, unfair added burden on the fund raising staff of the institution. In this case, the full board assumed the finance committee had fully exercised the responsibility delegated to it and thus approved the committee's recommendation for budget approval. For its part, the members of the finance committee assumed the staff was providing them with valid figures and may have felt they would be interfering if they questioned them. In fact, the members of the finance committee were derelict in their duty.

Other, particularly smaller-budget, institutions have faced serious fiscal problems when members of finance committees have not questioned and planned for the budget implications of staff positions funded by public funds – particularly positions integral to the operation of the institution that have been funded by CETA. Prudent planning and implementation of a finance committee's responsibility demands that when a staff position is created and is paid for by funds such as CETA, or other contributed funds, continued funding for such positions must be built into the future basic budget of the institution, or the position must be discontinued.

After the finance committee approval of the projected budget, the budget should be presented for full board approval by the chairman of the finance committee. *All members of the board must understand the budget, its purpose, and its implications.* Subsequent to full board approval of the budget, the finance committee must assume its monitoring responsibility. By this time, cash flow projections for the year, keyed to the budget, should have been presented by staff to the finance committee. Staff should provide the committee with regular (monthly or quarterly, depending upon the institution) reports of expenditures and income so that any deviation from projected income or expenditures will be seen prior to the development of a crisis situation. Based on actual experience as the fiscal year progresses, budget revisions may prove to be necessary and should be made prior to any fiscal crisis caused by shortfall in income or a more rapid rate of expenditure than planned, or both. In fact, staff of the institution should make the finance committee aware of any deviations from the budget. If staff does not do so on their own, it is the responsibility of the committee to note such changes and to assist the staff in coming to terms with the fiscal realities. If the committee does not do this, it is, as is the rest of the board, derelect in its duty.

No finance committee of a board can or should work in isolation from other committees whose activities are pertinent to the creation and implementation of the budget, e.g., the fund raising committee and the planning committee.

Fund Raising Committee The fund raising committee, or the development committee as some institutions call it, has a totally different functional purpose than the finance committee. It is surprising how many institutions, particularly smaller ones, combine the functions of finance and fund raising committees into one. They should be totally separate committees, although the work of each is important to the work of the other. *The fund raising committee has the ultimate responsibility for acquiring all, repeat all, of the contributed income necessary to the approved budget.* This responsibility should generally be divided into three sectors of committee activity: 1. deciding on the amount of contributed income possible to raise; 2. planning for the raising of contributed income; and 3. implementing those plans.

Most fund raising committees of not-for-profit professional performing arts institutions do not participate directly in the decision of how much money must be raised in a particular fiscal year. In many institutions this contributed income goal is, in fact, the swing figure plugged into the budget in order to make it appear balanced. It is a figure of contributed income needed, based on the assumption that projected earned income and expenditure figures are realistic. *It is imperative that the chairman or a member of the fund raising committee attend and participate in some finance committee discussions during the budget preparation stage so that he or she can help establish the projected contributed income budget figure.* The chairman of the fund raising committee will then be able to convey in more meaningful terms to the board as a whole the need for raising a particular amount of money for the year in order to implement the artistic purpose of the institution.

The contributed income category of the budget is integral to the institution's total successful operation. While the full board delegates its responsibility to the fund raising committee for the creation and implementation of the plan to attain the contributed income goal, *it should not delegate to the committee the final responsibility for the raising of the funds. The board as a whole must assist the committee in the implementation of its plans –* participating in the actual raising of the dollars necessary to offset the budgeted income gap. Not to do so places any individual non-participating trustee in the position of being derelict in his or her responsibility as an active board member. The only exception to this obligation is if an individual board member has an actual conflict of interest. If, for example, a trustee is responsible for the raising of funds for the institution of which he or she is a salaried employee, there could be an obvious conflict of interest if he or she approached the same sources for contributed funds for the not-for-profit professional performing arts institution of which he or she is a trustee. But despite such a conflict, there are ways for that individual trustee to provide fund raising assistance, at least indirectly, through professional advice and informal contacts.

The fund raising committee as a standing committee must meet on a regular basis to achieve its goals. With the staff support and assistance, the committee must develop strategies and plans for the raising of funds and set rigid timetables for the implementation of its plans, keyed to the fiscal necessities of the institution, particularly in relation to the projected periods of cash flow need. Responsibilities for the coordination of activities to achieve the fund raising goals should be assigned.

In a large number of institutions, the staff handles the work associated with obtaining grants from public sector donors: federal, state, county, and city. In many institutions the staff also does most, if not all, of the work associated with raising other contributed funds. It is in this broad area that boards should be much more active than they are. If the sources of contributed income are carefully identified, and if each category of source has an assigned goal (e.g., foundations, individuals, business and corporations, special events), then each of these source categories can be assigned to a member of the fund raising committee as that particular trustee's responsibility. This does not mean that trustee is responsible directly for raising all the money from the particular category. But he or she is responsible to see that the money is raised and raised on schedule. Subdividing the total amount to be raised by category of source, makes it more possible to create appropriate time tables for action and also makes possible a more reasonable estimate of the time necessary for each board member to participate in the total fund raising activity. Further, each will know precisely when during the course of the year that activity must take place.

Planning Committee   *A planning committee is vital to the continuing health and growth of an institution.* Thoughtful planning for the future provides staff and board with a rational proposed timetable for the introduction and/or implementation of programs designed to fulfill the purpose for which the institution exists. Assuming there is a clear definition of purpose, the planning committee can, with careful continuing study, recommend when certain programs should be introduced, rather than, as is so often the case, new programs evolving on a more or less ad hoc basis. Comprehensive planning also allows the programming to shape the budget, rather than having a predetermined level of budget dictate what activities are possible. The planning process establishes a rational basis for any change of programming to better implement the purpose of the institution. *Without planning, there is no context within which sound decisions may be made.*

A planning committee often is known as the long-range planning committee. For many organizations, planning for a year is a long-range plan. For others, it is possible to look three to five years ahead. Ideally, an institution should work toward being able to outline a plan covering at least a three-year period. Toward the middle, or at least well before the end of, the first year of a three-year plan, the current year should be updated in terms of what actually has occurred and what realistically is anticipated for the balance of the year. The second and third years should then be modified on the basis of achievement during the first year. By the end of the first year, another year is added to the far end of the plan so that there always is a period of three years projected.

Planning can only be done effectively where there is a clear understanding of the purpose of the institution. For example, if a dance company includes a school as part of its program, it should be clear what the purpose of the school is in relationship to the purpose of the company as an institution. Is the school primarily in existence to earn money to help subsidize the performances of the company? Or is it in existence primarily to provide continuing training for members of the company and to train potential company members? There is no right or wrong, but any decision should be based on an understanding of why the company exists and why the school should exist in terms of the basic purpose of the company. Understanding what the purpose of the school is will provide a base for clear decisions about it. If a theatre company or opera company exists to produce and perform classical works, is there any program validity to establishing workshops in contemporary scripts, libretti, or compositions?

The planning committee of a board should discuss all ideas in depth and assure the total institutional team how proposed new or modified programs fit into and support the implementation of the institution's purpose. If they don't fit in, then they should not be introduced. Or, the purposes of the institution should be modified in a conscious way.

Executive Committee   The executive committee is the standing committee that appears most often in institutional by-laws. It is also the one committee to which is and can be delegated all the powers of the board. *Usually when an executive committee exists, it is empowered to act on behalf of the full board between regular meetings of the board.* It is sound to have a mechanism in existence that can act rapidly when needed for some particular urgent institutional matter or problem. Many institutions also have found that a strong, small executive committee provides for truly efficient operation. But there is an inherent institutional danger when an executive committee assumes ongoing active responsibility for the institution. Trustees who are not members of the executive committee often feel left out of the decision-making process and may feel their primary function as a board member is to rubber stamp executive committee decisions.

It should be remembered clearly that although powers may be delegated to a committee by the full board, the full board still has the ultimate responsibility for all actions taken on its behalf. It cannot delegate that final responsibility. An executive committee acting in the name of the board is doing just that. It is acting in the name of the whole board, in the collective name of the trustees. If board members, not included on the executive committee, feel left out of the decision making process, there is not reason to expect they will be likely to be working members of the board. What difference do their efforts make if decisions are made without their participation in discussion or consultation? Why should they feel responsible for participating actively in fund raising if they do not really feel part of the institution for which they are supposed to raise the funds?

Delegation of authority or power does not mean abrogation of that power by the committee to which such authority is delegated. To preclude such, even though it normally may be an unconscious development based on efficiency, boards should provide at the very minimum that the minutes of executive committee meetings be distributed to all board members within a very short period of time after the committee has met. Further, unless it has been necessary for the executive committee to approve a contract or some other arrangement directly affecting a third party, *all actions taken by the executive committee in the name of the full board should be approved by the full board at its next regular or special meeting.* In this way, the board retains to itself the real power of action, while the executive committee acts formally in the name of the board only when immediate action really is necessary.

In the case of institutions that have large boards, e.g., some of the more established orchestral groups, theatres, operas, and large-budget dance companies, active use of the executive committee may be the only effective way of getting board business done. In such institutions, it might be wise to reconsider why the board is so large. If it is for special geographical reasons, or essentially for fund raising reasons, or if it is deemed necessary for any variety of reasons to have many so-called leading names on the board, then perhaps the governance of the institution should be restructured to better reflect the purpose of the large number of individuals involved. It might be better in such cases to create a large support group with appropriate honorific or dignified title and establish an actual board of a more limited, workable size. As will be discussed in the next chapter, there is no one simple answer to the question of what is the best size for a board of trustees. The point made here is that *the purpose and use of the executive committee should be clearly delineated by each institution, and its relationship to other committees and the full board should be equally clearly defined.*

In some institutions, all board committees report to the full board through the executive committee. In others, the executive committee is used in a limited way, with each board committee reporting directly to the full board. When standing committees are established in the by-laws of any institution, they normally are considered committees of the board, not committees of the executive committee. But in many cases, often due to the perceived need for more efficient board operation, committees are in fact considered, and become, committees of the executive committee, not of the board. Each institution should decide for itself what the real function of its executive committee is to be.

Volunteer Support Organizations and Committees   Institutions differ widely in their use of, and structural relation to, various types of volunteer support organizations and support committees, e.g., Friends of ---, Guilds, Angels. Some such groups are legally established as independent organizations. Some are provided for in the by-laws of the institutions and are legally an integral part of it. Some have no actual legal identity but pretend or assume they do, raising money and issuing receipts for donor income tax purposes without having the legal authority to do so. There are many valuable contributions and activities entered into by support groups, but it is essential that the relationship with the performing arts institution be clearly – and legally – defined. *No volunteer support groups should be established unless there is meaningful work for them to undertake and an appropriate staff/volunteer relationship established.*

The following has been prepared by Peter Donnelly, Producing Director of the Seattle Repertory Theatre, which has been particularly successful in establishing productive working relationships with its volunteer support group.

THE THEATRE, THE BOARD, AND ITS VOLUNTEERS
by Peter Donnelly

One of the phenomena that makes American arts institutions different from those in many other countries is that the governing bodies of our institutions are, in most cases, lay boards of trustees, bodies of individuals drawn from various professions and walks of life who commit themselves to overseeing the well-being of our institutions. Much discussion has been generated in the past few decades about this structure, questioning whether it is the one that best serves the arts and, more particularly, the artist. Variations on the structure have been tested, but the bottom line seems apparent: boards of trustees are here to stay, and, more importantly, are an integral and effective component of an institution *when their responsibilities are clearly outlined and their authority is defined.*

The Board of Trustees of the Seattle Repertory Theatre is limited by its by-laws to fifty people and, as the name implies, is responsible for the overall trusteeship of the theatre. By design, the board is meant to be representative of the Seattle community, and efforts are made to be certain the governing body reflects the variety of the city's people. In its own eyes, and in the eyes of the theatre's administration, the Rep Board is viewed as part of the "root system" of the organization – connecting the theatre to diverse areas of the community, all essential to the organization's growth and well-being. Of the fifty members serving on the board at any given time about thirty-five are truly active on an ongoing basis and serve on one or more committee(s). All of the trustees are volunteers who give of their time, expertise, and resources as called upon. This board has made it a policy not to involve itself in procedural matters or artistic considerations, but rather to deal with major policy questions of the theatre, matters of funding, and basic philosophical questions that surface from time to time. The board addresses questions such as, what should the institution do to serve the community? Are we doing it effectively? They also assist in specific projects, as well as confront ongoing questions of philosophy. As a matter of course, the board from time to time informally evaluates the staff, and, equally important, has found a mechanism for evaluating itself and how its responsibility to the institution is fulfilled.

A good many years ago a need was felt by the staff to have an informal discussion time with the board as a whole. A monthly meeting scheduled for an hour, or an hour and a half, was not the arena in which important philosophical questions could be considered in detail. The points of business and the reporting integral to the monthly meeting allotted little time for philosophy and for grappling with significant long-term questions. It was at this time that the suggestion for a day-long seminar or retreat was posed and enthusiastically adopted by the board. This has now become an annual event held on a Saturday or Sunday. The attendance by the board is excellent. The questions that cannot be dealt with in a monthly meeting, where time is limited, can be dealt with at the seminar, but no attempt is made to take action at the seminar. Rather, proposals are developed for the staff. The seminar also provides another very useful purpose. In the free discussion that ensues, the board is able to recognize that even within its own body there are dissenting opinions as to what direction should be taken on certain issues, thereby illustrating that out of these differing opinions some form of consensus must be arrived at by staff and board.

I do believe the communication between the management and board is helped by the informal discussions that take place within the seminar sessions. It is certainly valuable for the staff to hear feedback regarding a season or a production from individual board members, since very often the comments are a reflection of what the board member's colleagues feel about the theatre, and this opinion becomes useful information for weighing decisions.

Learning how to "read" the board is the responsibility of the staff. I find it comforting to know that the body encompasses a wide range of expertise, and that solutions to many of the important problems of the institution may be found among the people on that board.

Above and beyond the board of trustees, most organizations have a support group of one kind or another. In the case of the Seattle Rep, it is a guild of over 350 people who provide services and dollars to the operation of the theatre. The Seattle Repertory Organization (the women's guild) existed before the Seattle Repertory Theatre. When it was decided at the end of the Seattle World's Fair that a theatre company would be created, a women's auxiliary helped to merchandise the dream. Before the theatre ever opened, over 9,000 season tickets were sold for the first season – a remarkable feat. The vitality and devotion of that organization has been maintained for the past eighteen years. The remarkable thing is that as the character of the theatre itself has changed, the guild has adjusted itself to the institution's changing needs.

In the second or third season of the theatre, the by-laws of the organization were rewritten to assure the guild sufficient representation on the governing body of the theatre. Now the president of the guild and one elected guild member serve on the board to assure a clear and direct communication line to the board. This was an important step for the organization, because it appeared from time to time to guild members that significant policy matters were being discussed without input from the army of volunteers who serve. It also, of course, gives the guild direct access to the board, enabling them to enlist board support in guild activities that serve the theatre. This is a very important part of the root system of the organization – the numbers prove it out. We figure that 50 percent of the volunteers have spouses and that each volunteer has a circle of ten friends. Then the numbers start to have some real significance in terms of community penetration. Our experience has shown that time spent working with, and encouraging, volunteers comes back to us three-fold in human and financial resources, if motives and needs are clearly communicated.

Because of the number of volunteers directly involved with the theatre, we have had little cause to venture outside of that group for additional volunteer help. It is rare for us to appoint someone from outside the organization to board committees, except in the case of the nominating committee of the board, which allows for one at-large member from the community. Occasionally, a member of the community with a specific area of expertise will be consulted, but this is usually on a limited basis.

The women's guild of the theatre sponsors activities that generate funds for the operation to the same ends that the board of the theatre expects support from all of its constituents. They expect board support for guild activities and are not at all reticent in conveying that message. Current projects are discussed in the board meetings, sign-up sheets are circulated, commitments are extracted from the board members, and all-in-all the current activities are considered institution activities. This is good. The responsibility flows in both directions, and there is little questioning within either the guild or the board as to whether there will be mutual involvement. Rather, the question is: What will be the nature of the support and the degree? The atmosphere among the volunteers, both board and guild, is cordial, good natured, and mutually supportive.

Peter Donnelly
   Peter Donnelly has been Producing Director of the Seattle Repertory Theatre since 1970. He serves on the Boards of Trustees of the National Corporate Theatre Fund and the American Arts Alliance. He is a member of the University of Puget Sound's Board of Visitors for the Arts and the National Council for Boston University. Mr. Donnelly is the first recipient of the Washington Association of Theatre Artists President's Award for individual achievement in theatre.

Delegation of Responsibility to Staff   It has been repeated many times already in this manual that the board of trustees has the final responsibility for, and authority over, the institution. In the same way that it delegates some of this responsibility to board committees, while retaining ultimate responsibility as a board, it also normally delegates and should delegate operating responsibility to staff: to the artistic leadership for artistic affairs and to the management leadership for administrative affairs, whatever his or her specific title might be, e.g., managing director, producing director, general manager, executive director.
   In most instances, the only personnel of the institution who should be hired or fired by the board are the artistic director and the managing director. In the case of opera, there often are three top positions: the general director, the music director, and the stage director. All other artistic and administrative personnel should be hired by the artistic and management leadership, not by the board. In an institution that has been founded by an artistic leader, who also has created his or her board and also has hired the administrative leader, one normally does not anticipate the artistic director being fired by the board. But as institutions evolve, becoming stronger institutions per se, there may develop differences of opinion in regard to purpose and its implementation. Further, as budgets increase in size and increased levels of contributed income become necessary, trustees working for the institution may become disenchanted with the prospect of the same continued artistic leadership. If such becomes the case, and if there are enough trustees who feel strongly, it is possible for the artistic director to be eased out or dismissed. It also is possible for the disenchanted board members to resign. It is further possible, as happened in a leading theatre, for the artistic director to, in a sense, "fire" the board by departing the legal structure of the institution and establishing a new one.
   In delegating responsibility for the artistic affairs of the institution to the artistic leader or leaders, *the board is not, nor should it be, involved directly in the selection of the artistic season.* Any reasonable artistic director will share with the board the evolution of thought going into the creation of a season and the artistic rationale and vision underlying the final selections. In an institution where there is a healthy and creative relationship between the board and

the artistic leader, the individual trustees learn through the process of discussion (not just presentation) why an artistic season is, what it is, and how it relates to implementing the purposes of the institution. They also learn in advance, of any part of the season that might be, or might appear to be, a deviation from the accepted norm, what might be of an experimental nature, and the why of both. In turn, during the course of these discussions, the board members share with the artistic leadership any concerns they may have about the season in terms of the mores of the community in which the institution is located. But *the final responsibility for the actual selection of choreographic works, plays, operas, or musical compositions remains with the artistic leadership, not with the trustees.*

The board in fact exercises its authority through budget approval. Budget approval, however, should not be tied to disenchantment with one artistic choice. To offer a possible example: if an artistic director, in cooperation with the managing director, constructs a season based on a budget with a projected budget income gap larger than the board believes is capable of being met through contributed income, the board should not direct that "x" production be eliminated. Rather, it is up to the artistic director to establish artistic priorities and restructure his or her projected season within the limits of the budget discussed. If the resulting revised proposed season is far out of line with the perceived purposes of the institution, then either the artistic leader resigns or is dismissed, or the board resigns. The point here is that specific artistic decisions leading to implementation of the artistic mission through performance activities are the responsibility of the artistic director, not of the board.

The board also delegates considerable responsibility to the top management or administrative person who is responsible for the administrative aspects of the institution. *Management provides what is necessary to implement the artistic purpose of the institution.* As discussed above, a great deal of constructive advice and support can and should be provided by committees of the board, but the day-to-day management should be in the hands of the top-salaried management person on the staff. In the by-laws of many not-for-profit professional performing arts institutions, it is written that the president of the board is the chief executive officer or chief operating officer of the institution. This simply is not the case, nor should it be, in the not-for-profit sector. The chief executive officer or the chief operating officer in the for-profit corporation is normally the senior salaried individual who may well have the title of President. The president of the board of trustees of a not-for-profit institution is not a salaried person. Members of the board, as members, do not receive compensation. A salaried member of the institution also may be a member of the board of trustees, but he or she is paid a salary for the professional staff position (e.g., as artistic director or managing director), not as a trustee. *Depending on the*

*nature of the institution, the chief executive officer may be either the
artistic or the management leader, but not the president of the board
of trustees.*

Three contributions discussing "working" boards follow. The first, "The 'Working' Board of Trustees" was written by Robert H. Craft, Jr., a Trustee of The Washington Opera and a Washington, D.C. attorney. The second, "Examples of Working Boards" was prepared by Philip Semark, Managing Director of the Joffrey Ballet, formerly with the San Francisco Ballet. The third, "The Magic of a Working Board" was contributed by David R. Patterson, a Trustee of Ballet Metropolitan in Columbus, Ohio.

THE "WORKING" BOARD OF TRUSTEES
by Robert H. Craft, Jr.

A "working" board of trustees of an arts institution – whether theatre, opera, ballet, or museum – offers tremendous advantages and poses certain hazards, over a non-working, or honorary board. By exploiting the advantages and avoiding the pitfalls, an arts institution can derive significant strength from a working board that organizations with solely honorary boards do not enjoy.

The ways in which a "working" board can contribute to the strength of the organization are limited only by the imagination of its leadership and the dedication of its members. Recent experiences of the Board of Trustees of The Washington Opera provide illustrative examples of the ways in which the energies of individual board members may be productively channeled.

My definition of a "working" board is one where each member – or at least a substantial majority of the members – contributes individual effort to the success of the institution beyond mere attendance at board meetings or the making of financial contributions. At the outset I should offer my personal view, however, that there is one way in which the board should not work – it should not attempt to second-guess the day-to-day operations and artistic judgment of the institution's professional management. Although the board is, of course, ultimately responsible for the success or failure of the organization, I believe that the best way to exercise that responsibility is to engage the best professional management possible, to develop policies for and provide guidance to that management, and thereafter to rely on the management to execute the artistic decisions.

This does not mean that board members should not be involved in the operations of the company when needed. In fact, many members of the board of The Washington Opera are called upon weekly by the professional management for assistance in a wide variety of ways. Businessmen provide advice on financing alternatives, cost control, and long-term planning; a partner of a professional accounting firm advises in connection with the establishment of an accounting system; the head of a management systems firm provides expertise on computerizing of subscription information, ticket sales and related matters; lawyers on the board assist in negotiating lease space and the drafting of contracts with suppliers; government relations experts provide advice in dealing with the federal government and endowment organizations; and others with expertise or contacts assist in obtaining warehouse space for production storage, construction forms for creation of scenery, and printing and paper firms for brochures – i.e., the members of the board are "working" by contributing in the areas of their expertise, in many cases expertise that the organization could not afford to buy.

All board members need not be experts in order to make a meaningful contribution. In fact, the most important mission of a working board is fund raising, and at The Washington Opera every member of the board – some 40 to 50 individuals – is expected to serve on at least one committee: foundations, major gifts ($1,000 and over), special gifts (up to $1,000), or corporate gifts. The donation of time is the greatest contribution a board member can make, since, as we all know who have tried it, fund raising is nothing if not time-consuming. Faced with apparent federal budget cuts affecting government support for all the arts, the working board member as a fund raiser will become increasingly indispensable. Generally, to be an effective fund raiser, you must first make a contribution yourself; in fact, a substantial commitment by the individual trustees of an organization is generally regarded by foundations as a necessary pre-condition to any grant to an arts organization. Our rule at the Washington Opera is that each board member is expected to contribute a specified minimum amount annually or, in certain cases where financial constraints make this difficult, to be responsible for contributions from new sources in an equivalent amount.

I conclude from this that one of the most important characteristics of a successful working board is diversity of membership – united by the common characteristic of a commitment to the organization evidenced by a willingness to donate time and effort and not just money or prestige. Our professional management has told me that one of the most important and constructive contributions the board members have made in recent years is instilling in the professional management the feeling that the board members are always available to be called upon when needed – whether it be for business, legal or accounting advice or an introduction to a foundation or a corporation. It is this individual commitment of time and energy by board members that makes a working board really "work".

Robert H. Craft, Jr.
Robert H. Craft, Jr., a lawyer in private practice with the Washington office of a New York law firm, is a trustee of The Washington Opera and Chairman of its Special Gifts Committee. Born in New York City, he is a graduate of Princeton University; University College, Oxford; and Harvard Law School. He currently resides in Chevy Chase, Maryland.

EXAMPLES OF WORKING BOARDS
by Philip Semark

The prime function of any board of trustees of a not-for-profit organization is to provide informed and appropriate guidance to the artistic directors and management of the organization, to set policy, and to effectively plan its implementation.

The main program or vehicle available to any board of trustees is the development and approval of the budget. The budget, as presented by an institution's administration, outlines proposed programs and expenditures – together with projection of income, both contributed and earned. The revenue gap that has to be funded by contributed income should provide the main focus for the board of trustees. The board of trustees is responsible for the institution as a whole – both in the short and long-term. Moreover, they have to undertake to raise the necessary funds to balance the budget adequately and to fund raise to meet the goals suggested by the administration.

In addition, the board of trustees must examine closely the expenditures of the organization to ensure that monies, both earned and contributed, are spent effectively and wisely. Any document as complex as a budget cannot and should not be examined by a full board. More properly, the responsibility of examining a budget has to be delegated by the chairman or president of a board to a budget and finance committee which, as a small and intimate group, can accomplish the task. Their duties will be not only to examine the budget prior to its presentation to the full board for approval, but also to examine its ongoing management throughout the fiscal year to ensure that any variances encountered through the year are anticipated and met by contributed income or budget cutbacks.

One of the major programs, in fact the primary program of any board of trustees, must be an effective and successful development campaign. This function, again, in any large organization remains too complex to be left in the hands of a large board; it must be delegated to a development committee. It must be emphasized repeatedly by the management and board leadership, however, that development remains a prime responsibility of the board as a whole – although its planning and specific implementation must be delegated to the development committee (under the leadership of one of the board's officers) working in conjunction with a professional development staff.

The administration of an institution has the responsibility of developing sound and accurate projections of contributed income, as well as suggesting ways to maximize a contributed income effort to bring in new and increased funding. The responsibilities of the development committee extend beyond the mere planning and implementation of the fund raising plan, to the actual participation of its members and those of other relevant board members in the programmatic aspect of the development campaign. Trustees have access to corporate, foundation, and private individuals as peers, enabling them to make personal calls to effect a development discussion with an appropriate staff member (either the chief executive officer, or the development manager, where appropriate).

Having ensured that both the budget and development aspects of the company are in place, the board's third main responsibility must be the long-range health of the organization. This can be divided into two main areas: that of long-range planning and that of ensuring the continuing leadership that will guide the institution in future years. This is accomplished by an effective and imaginative nominating committee composed of the present leadership of the board, together with newer board members.

Their task is not only to seek out the future leadership of the board, in terms of corporate and social leaders, but more importantly in the 1980s, to ensure that all economic, ethnic, and community sectors of the city, or region that the institution serves, are adequately and properly represented on the board.

The long-term future of the institution must necessarily be the responsibility of the long-range planning committee. It is charged with both developing a short and long-term strategy for the institution and the programs and policies by which such strategy will be implemented. This committee should meet periodically with the senior management staff to formulate a plan that the institution takes as its point of departure. The present situation of the institution must be merged with the vision of the artistic director of the institution as it may be three, five, ten, or even twenty years ahead.

The financial realities of such a plan must be addressed, together with the realities of the earned and contributed income base required to support such a vision. This results in a comprehensive plan such as the one that the San Francisco Ballet has used effectively – with the private, corporate, and government sectors – to articulate to those various constituencies that problems had, in fact, been addressed in a realistic and financially feasible method.

Once such a plan is in place, it remains the responsibility of the long-range planning committee to monitor and update the plan accordingly, preferably at two to three-year intervals.

From time to time, the chairman or president of the board may see fit to appoint ad hoc committees to address specific problems that face an organization. For example, the planning and implementation of a capital fund raising campaign for obtaining new facilities would require the establishment of such a committee. It is sometimes useful to designate such a committee the "Office of the Chairman" out of which various subcommittees would be drawn. The advantage of having such a committee carry the title of "Chairman" is that it lends additional weight to the project and indicates its importance – both to the internal staff and the external world. Such a committee that works on a finite project also provides good training ground for future board leaders where their performance may be monitored under controlled circumstances by other members of the board. Capital campaigns provide the most useful example of the utilization of the special ad hoc committee. A committee to raise or increase an endowment may be another important example. In conclusion, these standing and ad hoc committees are the vehicles by which a board implements its purposes and, as such, may be termed their programs.

One last general purpose that remains the responsibility of the board (which encompasses all of the above committees) is to articulate and represent the organization's missions and objectives to the outside world. While this must necessarily remain part of the focus of the artistic administration and management, the board – by its definition and composition – remains an important conduit for the organization to speak to its community, its peer group, and its fund raising constituency.

Philip Semark

Philip Semark is Executive Vice President of The Joffrey Ballet. Prior to this he spent five years as the General Manager of the San Francisco Ballet. He served as President of the Board of Trustees of Performing Arts Services, Inc. (New York, NY) and as a member of the Charter Committee of the Friends of Fort Mason (San Francisco, CA). He was a member of the California Arts Council Dance Advisory Panel and a board member of Hospital Audiences, Inc. Mr. Semark is currently a member of the Managers of Larger Dance Companies Committee and the Board of Trustees of The Foundation for the Joffrey Ballet.

THE MAGIC OF A WORKING BOARD
by David R. Patterson

Something very new, refreshing, and exciting came to Columbus three years ago in the form of Ballet Metropolitan! Having been an arts appreciator and participant for many years, ballet never entered my mind as an integral part of this wonderful and enjoyable field that has played such an important role in our world's history. Professional ballet was not a part of the Columbus scene – so it never really existed for me. Though our family interests in the main had gone far beyond our community, cultural interests and responsibilities stopped at the city limits, or so it seemed.

Two and one-half years ago, several extremely dedicated young women approached me to join the Board of Ballet Metropolitan. Although I had heard of this developing company – in that one of these women had contacted me the previous two years for contributions – I was not at all thrilled with the "opportunity" offered to help salvage what appeared to be a loser. No one likes to be associated with a loser in any community when winning is the name of the game. And how could professional ballet possibly become a winner in Columbus, Ohio, when our symphony, art museum, and dramatics organizations after years of operation were still finding it difficult to maintain bottom-line black figures even with the fine products and management they provided? Our own popular and highly respected mayor only rated the city as grade B, sometimes B+, when truly it is a great community, though not known for its desire to embrace new charitable or cultural organizations. Long story short – the women were indeed so persuasive and evidenced such commitment that I had to accept the challenge. We sorely needed professional ballet to fully round out our arts colony – and they were absolutely right.

Attending the fall concert shortly thereafter with 200 others (in the 3,000 seat Ohio Theatre), my wife and I were most impressed with the pure grace and artistic excellence of the dancers and the utter relaxing tranquility of the entire evening. Critics were saying, "Where are the people?" We were saying, "See it once and you'll never miss another opportunity!" Obviously we were sold on professional ballet and Ballet Metropolitan, in particular, for Columbus. I was now a fully licensed, dedicated board member, ready to run out and sell our ballet to the world. With a generous matching grant of $200,000 from Battelle Memorial Institute Foundation over three years (1978-80) to establish Ballet Met as a fully professional ballet company, we achieved the support to reach our objective.

New board members carefully selected from a variety of important fields were added, bringing with them increased resources. Working as a team with our artistic director, a total reevaluation of priorities resulted in a higher performance quality. This translated into our nine "Nutcracker" performances for the 1980 Christmas season, averaging slightly over 90 percent attendance. We were in the black for the second consecutive year.

Before it begins to look like we accomplished this entirely on our own, it should be pointed out that FEDAPT's management technical assistance was an important component in this reevaluation process. The one and one-half day retreat in September 1980 with FEDAPT consultants as facilitators saw 90 percent of our trustees in attendance. This experience was extremely valuable to us at that stage of our development.

Our outstanding past and present board presidents forged such splendid programs and set such inspirational work examples that you felt a deep sense of guilt if you did not eat, sleep, and think Ballet Met. I had seen board commitment previously, but never to this degree. Leadership motivates and supplies the magic of a working board.

With the advent of the propsed cuts in the National Endowment for the Arts' appropriation, and the possiblility that there may well be even further reductions as we proceed into the 1980s, it behooves all of us as trustees to search diligently for new sources of contributed income from the private sector (individuals, foundations, corporations, etc.) if we are to successfully implement our Ballet Metropolitan programs and activities. Simultaneously, it will be mandatory to put more pressure on earned income to carry a larger percentage burden of our total revenues; and finally, expenses will have to be more closely controlled to complete the cycle.

To assist in these accomplishments, our products and services must continue to improve, and our "packaging" of them should be made more attractive, entertaining, and exciting each year. These are all facts – not startling to anyone – but the facts for everyone associated with the arts for the years ahead. Since time and space limits thorough discussion of details surrounding these basics of any operation, please permit me to dwell a moment on the issues of implementing the funding of our Ballet Met, for without private dollars to support our programs we would not be in business!

As mentioned, our real professional life is only three years old – we are currently embarking on our third annual operating fund drive. We made a grievous error in our initial campaign two years ago. I hope this account of that experience will serve to help others avoid making a similar mistake.

We opted to have our 1979 campaign run for eighteen months from January 1979 through June 1980. Most businesses are on a calendar year and establish their contributions and other budgets on such a basis. Confusion arose with some major corporate donors in the 1980 campaign that followed, in that they contended their first-year gift actually covered both 1979 and 1980. Though our 1980 campaign was more successful than the 1979 eighteen-month effort, we lost some credibility (and dollars) with certain firms and individuals of those organizations through this ill-chosen initial campaign approach. The ending was a happy one, however, as follow-up explanatory contacts with these corporations removed the stigma and put us back in their good graces. Our future campaigns should have clear sailing. Moral: Always design your fund raising efforts to suit your contributors' convenience and practices.

Eighty-five percent of our eighteen members personally support our campaigns and about the same percentage have worked as solicitors on our fund raising drives, many as divisional heads in each of our campaigns. For success, a high degree of board participation in this area is absolutely mandatory.

The requested board member commitment to the 1980 campaign was that each would be responsible for raising $1,500, with their personal gifts representing no less than $150 of this figure. (Committing your own "blood, sweat, and tears" dollars first makes one a much more effective solicitor.) Our board dramatically exceeded the $42,000 commitment on the basis described above and averaged approximately $400 each in their personal gifts. (Our members, with few exceptions, are not affluent.) Our 1980-81 budget was $85,000 and we raised $122,000 in our 1980 campaign. Board members were responsible for 78 percent of these dollars. What more can one ask? I think this is exemplary performance by our board volunteers, particularly when we have no development director and our managing director has to cover both assignments.

It should be pointed out that earned income was 53 percent in 1980 and should rise to 65 percent in 1981. A challenge grant from the Columbus Foundation based on earned income improvement inspired us toward further excellence in this vital area.

This year we continue to have the same board involvement in our campaign but have been able to obtain more outside executive participation from local leaders. We are emphasizing our fine track record, and we are asking men and women to get involved with a young and exciting organization – one truly moving up in the arts community in our city. Our goal is to raise $150,000, though we are actually shooting for $200,000 of a projected $680,000 budget. We are featuring an extensive campaign that we believe will nullify any effects of the economy – one which includes the wearing of a ballet symbol by all board members and solicitors during the campaign. Special cocktail parties and receptions are featured for present as well as potential donors. A phonathon evening conducted by the "Friends of Ballet Met" will wrap up the fourth-quarter push. The top leadership of our fund raising campaign all three years has come from within our board membership.

Our youthful Pro-Met Women's Auxiliary plays a leading role as a support force. The two recent presidents of this group have molded a dynamic organization that will supply the future leadership of Ballet Met.

We now have in place our own Ballet Met Dance Academy, with over 300 students participating in the first six months of existence. Again, board members were the architects of this venture, and it is more than paying its way while serving our community.

Talk about a board that deals with reality, that faces up to its responsibilities, that is sensitive to the needs of Columbus – the Ballet Met Board does it all!

David R. Patterson

David R. Patterson is Chairman of the Board of Trustees of Ballet Metropolitan (Columbus, OH). Before retiring in 1981, he served as Vice Chairman of the Huntington National Bank, where he remains on the Board. Prior to this he was President of the Midwestern District of Borden, Inc. He currently serves as a board member of the Mid-Ohio Health Care Plan, Ohio Public Expenditure Council, Goodwill Industries, Central State University, Riverside Methodist Hospital, and St. Augustine's College. Mr. Patterson is a principal advisor and trustee to the E.F. Wildermuth Foundation and an advisor to the Columbus Foundation. He is the 1981 Chairman of the Executive Committee of United Negro College Fund, Inc. and is a past Vice Chairman and General Campaign Chairman for United Way.

Chapter 3

Structuring a Board

Size   There is no right or wrong size for a board of trustees of a not-for-profit professional performing arts institution.

The following contribution was prepared by William Stewart, Managing Director of The Hartford Stage Company in Hartford, Connecticut.

THE SIZE OF THE BOARD
by William Stewart

A board of trustees of five members may be too large if each one has not been selected for specific capabilities, leadership strengths, interest in the institution, and a willingness to commit meaningful time and support. A board of eighty will be too small if each member brings to it some singular expertise, the ability to provide special access, or significant financial resources.

The response most frequently heard to the question regarding the proper size of a board of trustees is "the size to get the job done." Of course, the immediate problem with this answer is that many performing arts institutions have not defined "the job to be done." The size of the board is often a function of the maturity of the institution. A newly founded organization is initially going to attract a limited number of people to serve. This is particularly true if the goals and operational needs of the company have not been firmly established. The more clearly the institution can articulate its role in the community and its relationship to various segments to that community, the simpler will be the task of determining board size and composition.

A professional theatre may start up in a community either as a result of an artist or manager assembling a small group of interested citizens or of the transition from an amateur theatre to a professional operation. In the latter situation, a board of trustees usually is in existence. It may also be too large. An amateur theatre board is large because much of the work of producing and marketing plays is assumed by volunteers, with board members responsible for very specific duties.

In both instances, the definition of the responsibilities of board members should be the task of the board leadership and the management of the institution. As this planning continues, the small board will undoubtedly expand and the larger board may be reduced in size.

In the winter 1972 issue of *California Management Review,* Ichak Adizes suggests that optimum board size should be fifteen to twenty-five members. For a developing institution these numbers are probably appropriate. With maturity it is entirely reasonable that a board might expand to a considerably larger number. If there is purposeful growth to fifty or even one hundred members, the leadership must recognize that such size presents specific problems of meaningful individual involvement and management. Such a large board may be totally appropriate for a very complex and big institution or one with wide geographical interests. In such an institution, a sophisticated and broad-based committee structure would be imperative. Meetings would need to be carefully planned and executed. A thorough analysis must have been made of the specific strengths of each member and the use to be made of them.

The size of a board is most usually defined in the by-laws of the company. In 1963, the Hartford Stage Company was incorporated, and the board of trustees to manage the property and affairs of the corporation was to number not less than seven nor more than sixty. In 1976, a by-law amendment increased that number to seventy-five.

The first board of the company consisted of eleven individuals from the community and the two professionals who founded the organization. These original members were asked to join for different reasons. Some were solicited because of their involvement with the ownership of the facility planned for the theatre. Some were selected for their status in the community and others because of their interest in the art of the theatre.

Membership continued to expand in an orderly manner until 1968 when financial crisis led to a reorganization of the board. The new leadership recognized the need for a broad base of community support and increased access to the corporate community. In the fall of 1969, the board was expanded to forty-five members. By 1974, that number had grown to over sixty members.

Board of trustee development is a continuing responsibility of the management and leadership of an institution. As the organization matures, it is very easy to become sloppy in maintaining the involved participation and renewal of board membership. Many by-laws provide for some system of rotating members off a board after a specified period of time. Such rotation must be maintained. It is very true that no one is indispensible. However, the concern that a board cannot continue to function without a specific individual frequently prevents the orderly rotation of old members. It is the responsibility of the nominating committee to be very tough in removing members when their terms expire.

In the late 1970s, the Hartford Stage Company Board became lax in implementing the three-year rotation rules. As a result, the board continued to have members who were no longer interested or effective. To bring on fresh, new, involved members, it became necessary to expand the Board to nearly seventy members. In this instance, the Board became too large.

Even when a mature institution has the "ideal" leadership, if it is a healthy institution well rooted and involved in its community, it should be understood that the leadership must continue on a regular basis. The best board member should be looking for his or her own replacement.

There is no objective formula for determining the size of a board of trustees. The ultimate size must be based on the effective and efficient use of people. The best number will become apparent once the needs of the institution are properly assessed and the criteria for membership is clearly established.

William Stewart

William Stewart has been Managing Director of the Hartford Stage Company since 1976 and held the same position there from 1969 to 1973. During the intervening three years he was Managing Director of the American Shakespeare Theatre, Stratford, Connecticut, where he had begun his career in 1962 as a Ford Foundation administrative intern. In 1967 Mr. Stewart went to the Cincinnati Playhouse as Managing Director. He has been a lecturer in theatre administration at the Yale School of Drama since 1974 and was appointed to the faculty in 1981. He has served as a consultant for FEDAPT for seven years and as a co-director of their Theatre Middle Management Program for five years.

Criteria for Board Membership   Board members and staffs of not-for-profit professional performing arts institutions spend a considerable amount of time discussing the apparent unwillingness of many board members to function as they should or as expected. There are constant questions about why boards don't function well, how best to energize them, or how to make them better working boards. Some trustees join a board and then are disappointed in not being used properly by their colleagues or the staff. Some staffs are seriously disappointed at the seeming lack of interest in the institution by board members and their resulting lack of work for the institution. Further, there often is disappointment in regard to trustee personal dollar contributions, if any, and the apparent serious reluctance of some to participate in fund raising. The question is, why?

Quite simply, *board members usually are not told what is expected of them when they join a board* and, in many cases, boards and staffs don't really know what they expect as a minimum degree of participation by board members. There are general ideas about this, but in all too few instances is there a clearly articulated set of minimum requirements for board membership. While each institution has its own, perhaps different, specific needs in terms of type and degree of service and support from the members of its board, *there are five basic criteria for trusteeship that each board should consider adopting.* If these criteria, or at least some criteria, are accepted as what is minimally expected from each trustee, each potential trustee should be so informed prior to joining the board. Further, each current trustee should consider his or her commitment to the institution in terms of the stated criteria. While it is suggested that the following criteria are the minimum to be expected from each trustee, exceptions may of course be made if there is an overriding conscious reason for doing so. For example a trustee may be able to fulfill most criteria but have a valid reason for not being able to satisfy all, e.g., there may be a real conflict of interest in fund raising. Nevertheless, *the following five criteria might well be considered as basic guidelines for board membership.*

1. Each trustee is expected to believe in and to be an active advocate of the institution.
2. Each trustee is expected to *subscribe* to the performances of the institution and to *attend* performances.
3. Each trustee is expected to attend board meetings.
4. Each trustee is expected to serve actively on at least one standing committee of the board.
5. Each trustee is expected to be *both* a dollar *giver* and a dollar *getter*.

There is absolutely no reason for an individual to accept election as a trustee of any institution in which he or she does not believe; or for which he or she cannot be an active advocate. If there is no belief in the value and importance of the institution, why should a trustee assume the obligations and responsibilities of trusteeship? If a trustee does not believe in the institution, how can he or she be an advocate of it?

It is not enough for a trustee to purchase a subscription. He or she also should attend the performances. If a trustee does not attend and experience the work performed firsthand, how can he or she know the product well enough to be an advocate of and for it? If trustees are not subscribers, how can effective subscription sales campaigns be mounted? If the governing body of the institution does not support performance through ticket purchase and attendance, why should they believe others in the general public will?

When a trustee accepts election to a board, he or she should expect to attend board meetings. If informed of this obligation ahead of time, and if the regular meetings of the board are scheduled a year in advance, there is no normal reason for non-attendance. It should be understood, however, that there will be times when attendance is not possible due to unexpected occupational or personal business conflicting with a regularly scheduled board meeting. Normally, however, attendance can and should be expected.

In addition to attending board meetings, each trustee will become a working member of the board if he or she serves actively on at least one of the board's standing committees. The key words are "actively" and "at least one." This is the minimal acceptable requirement. It is the least that should be expected of one who has accepted the responsibility of trusteeship. If a schedule of meetings of each of the standing committees is prepared a year in advance, based on what is really needed by the institution from that committee, then the time commitment of the trustee is more clearly defined and can more reasonably be integrated into his or her schedule.

Finally, each trustee is expected to give dollars to the institution and to help raise dollars. *This is not give or get. It is give and get.* There is disagreement among many in regard to how much a trustee is expected to give. Some argue that each trustee should be expected to give "x" amount of dollars — a set figure for all. Others argue, including the compiler of this manual, that each trustee should give what he or she feels able to give. There obviously is no absolute right or wrong in this, but *the important factor is that there is giving by 100 percent of the trustee body.* There are many individuals who can make valuable contributions to an institution through active service on the board, but who are not able to contribute dollars in any substantial sense. Their particular expertise or general knowledge may be of far greater importance than a given amount of dollar contribution. Such individuals should not be precluded from board service. On the other hand, every individual is able to provide some cash contribution, so the 100 percent board contribution goal can be attained. It is of enormous importance to many donors to know that all board members believe strongly enough in an institution to support it to at least some degree with personal dollar contributions. If such evidence of support does not come from the trustees as a whole, why should another donor feel interested in contributing?

Whether or not these five criteria for board membership are accepted, *some clearly defined criteria should be agreed upon and established by formal resolution of the board of each institution.* In this way, each prospective or current member of the board will know up front what is the minimum commitment expected. This should help preclude disappointments in regard to board service. Expectations will be clear.

The following contribution has been prepared by Barbara Hauptman, former Executive Director of the Twyla Tharp Dance Foundation.

RECRUITING BOARD MEMBERS: INDIVIDUAL TYPES AND TALENTS
by Barbara Hauptman

I am assuming that all who read this have come to terms with their artistic contributions and are looking to strengthen their niche in the performing arts industry by creating a useful and dynamic board of trustees. A board of trustees, no matter how good, will never camouflage mediocre quality or artistically propel an organization forward. Boards need to be custom-made by loving hands, and preferably of raw materials rather than synthetics. The shape and form must fit its function. The function must define its membership. A board is not paste-on; it is an integral, working component and the fine line between a resourceful institution and a struggling collection of talented individuals.

In forming a new organization or expanding the board of an established institution, it is imperative to define the board's goals and purposes. A prospectus that spells out the responsibilities of its members can be a very useful tool for recruiting new candidates and serve as a valuable document to current members as an expressed definition of their responsibilities. If the board's mandate is to raise money, actors, dancers, and musicians will be at a loss. If the board is to encourage arts advocacy, a marketing expert may not grasp the urgency of the issue. At the Twyla Tharp Dance Foundation, Inc., we had a prerequisite for board membership: an annual commitment of $10,000 to be given personally or raised from other sources. This requirement had to be carefully spelled out to each potential member so that there were no misunderstandings at a later date. The Cleveland Ballet has issued a very thorough manual for its trustees that includes such areas as the company's history, organizational structure, and detailed duties of trustees as they relate to the overall administration of the company. Board members should be challenged and stimulated by a clear understanding of their role, and organizations should be in better positions to utilize their boards more effectively.

Once the function of the board is outlined, diversity in the skills and contacts of the individuals represented can be crucial to its success. A board, like a good salad, should contain an assortment. Members should be chosen for their business strength and professional expertise. In looking at potential board members, professionals such as lawyers and accountants make valuable additions as they can often provide technical advise and donated services. Bankers and investment advisers may have numerous contacts within the philanthropic community and can guide an organization through the handling of money, loan procedures, and banking formalities. A real estate developer or architect can be utilized to explore space, relocation, or renovation expenses, since most arts organizations seem to be perpetually in search of bigger and better facilities. A board member familiar with the real estate market, coupled with the banker, the attorney, and the accountant, can guide any expansion more. However, no board needs a multiplicity of members in any one area of expertise.

At the Twyla Tharp Dance Foundation and the Urban Arts Corps Theater, space was the proverbial dilemma. We were never able to gather enough knowledgeable resources on the respective boards to "demystify" the intricacies of acquiring a new facility. The responsibility of acquiring new space without major board understanding and involvement was too burdensome for management alone; representatives from real estate development, or urban planning could have saved considerable time, energy, and money.

People who know people also make excellent trustees. The

"socialite" who is genuinely fond of the work of a company can interest a sphere of people in attending performances, hosting benefits, and contributing time and money. If interest in a company is the direct result, all the better for future fund raising.

The social aspects of board life may be repugnant to an artist, but his or her involvement with the board should be carefully cultivated. This opportunity for board members to meet artists can be an alluring feature of membership.

What's in a name? Glamor perhaps, Cachet. Often there is nothing of tangible substance in having a celebrity or household name sitting on your board. Perhaps some potential board members will be attracted to your organization by a "name," but eventually they will either want to meet him/her or will ask you to detail his/her contribution to the workings of the organization. Therefore, a "name" for the letterhead can often be a wasted board seat. A good working board demands time and active participation from its members. Stars, politicians, and ultra tycoons are often too busy or overcommitted. Stars are the most cumbersome; they have their own careers to promote and usually only lend their names. If they send a check with great regularity, then a board seat may be justifiable.

As the Executive Director of a performing arts organization, I always wanted board members to return my calls, comment on my decisions, and serve as a sounding board in critical matters. I did not like feeling as if I were intruding or imposing. Therefore, I strongly advise careful thought before inviting celebrities to join the board. Their motives for joining can be perfectly honorable and your desire to have them administratively sound. In reality, however, the frustration can outweigh the prestige.

In most cases, a theatre or dance artistic director is the driving force behind his/her company and often the architect of the group's style and approach to the art form. Artistic directors know the direction the company is heading and should have a board seat so that they can have a voice and a vote. With the addition of the artistic director to the other professionals you have identified that make up the board, all the indigenous elements of running a performing arts institution can come into play.

Staff members (other than artistic directors) on the board are not conducive to the interaction vital to the board's relationship with management. The dialogue process often can get stunted. The board and management staff must remain separate entities to ensure that all vantage points are represented. A management representative should be present at all board meetings *in a non-voting capacity* to avoid management staff being placed in a schizophrenic position.

In summary, board members should fulfill a designated function. They should be capable professionals in their fields and eager to grapple with the responsibilities and liabilities of board involvement. They should be able to relate to each other and to the staff. Bad chemistry or personality difficulties on a board are not only unpleasant, but all too often lead to a lack of productivity. Each prospective board member should be thoroughly researched and carefully scrutinized, as a bad choice can be very debilitating. The process of acquiring a new member should, in some ways, be as arduous as getting rid of an unsatisfactory one. Board members and organizations have a relationship akin to a marriage — so be sure to tread carefully during the courtship.

Barbara Hauptman

Barbara Hauptman is the Director of Operations of the Theatre Development Fund. Ms. Hauptman joined the Twyla Tharp Dance Foundation as Executive Director in August 1979. She produced *Twyla Tharp on Broadway* in 1980 and assisted in *Confessions of a Corner Maker,* CBS/Cable. From 1976 to 1979 she was an arts analyst in the Theatre Program for the New York State Council on the Arts. She was Managing Director for the Urban Arts Corps Theatre and the Bill Baird Marionettes as well as cofounder of Management Services for the Performing Arts. At the Williamstown Theatre Festival, she was General Manager for two summer seasons and coordinated the festival's participation in the PBS "Theatre in America" presentation of *The Seagull.* She is on the board of The Second Stage Company in New York City. Ms. Hauptman earned her M.F.A. at the Yale School of Drama.

Recruitment of Board Members   Structurally, the responsibility for the identification and nomination of members of a board of trustees lies with the nominating committee of the board. *The nominating committee should be a standing board committee. It should meet on a regular basis throughout each year to assess and discuss the needs of the board:* what types of members are needed and what particular expertise is necessary for the good of the institution.

Frequently, however, the identification, selection, and recruitment of board members occurs in a somewhat ad hoc way. The following is a not an unusual scenario. Sometime before the annual meeting, the nominating committee (if there is one) convenes, or a nominating committee is appointed. The members of the committee think of names of friends or names of prominent individuals in the community who presumably would be good to have as board members. Some think those being discussed might be too busy to accept. Some wonder if they really are approachable. Usually, it is decided to ask all members of the board to submit names of potential board candidates to the committee. Few on the board actually do this.

The next time the committee meets, it goes over the names in hand and decides, for a variety of reasons, who might be the best – or best attainable – candidates. A slate is then recommended to the board for approval and often an individual is elected to board membership without ever having been sounded out in advance in regard to interest. If this happens, the newly elected board member is approached by the president or chairman of the board, by the artistic or management leadership, or by a person on the board who knows him or her best, and is then asked to accept election. For some reason, many people do not reject such an offer even though they have not been sounded out in advance in regard to their interest, and even though they have no idea in any detail of what is expected of them once they become trustees.

Another scenario, particularly with newer institutions, might be the following. It is decided that it is time for the board to expand its membership beyond the few relatives or friends who agreed to participate in the original or founding board of the institution that evolved primarily out of the artistic impulse and need of a particular artist. Normally, by this time in the institution's history, the board and the small artistic and management staff have met and passed through the varied institutional developmental crises and are facing the possibility or necessity of increasing performance activities and possibly upgrading the level of salaries of the artists and staff. Often, all involved are quite tired, having worked hard and having attended and participated in many long board meetings that increasingly seem to be tied to budget problems.

Groups such as the above tend to worry about approaching others to help out. They doubt that individuals who are not friends would be willing to give service as board members and hesitate to ask others to do the institution a favor by joining the board. This attitude often precludes them from identifying carefully the needs of the institution that can be helped by carefully selected board members and inhibits them from approaching the particular individuals they may wish to recruit to the board, because they think it is asking too much.

Boards and staffs such as these are really forgetting three basic factors: 1. no one should prejudge another's interest or potential interest in joining a board; 2. people should have the privilege of saying yes or no, rather than someone saying it for them; and 3. it is where the interest of the institution and the interest of the potential or actual trustee come together that a creative and constructive relationship can develop. No one except the individual in question should determine where his or her interests lie and what membership on a board could provide in terms of satisfying those interests. *When an individual is invited to become a member of a board, the institution if not really asking a favor, it is offering a favor.*

There are many variations on the above scenarios, but it is quite rare to find an institution seriously assessing its needs that might be satisfied through the human resources of potential board members, and which then recruits members in a manner consistent with the best interests of the institution and its further development.

The following is suggested as a guideline for the more effective recruitment of board members. The nominating committee meets regularly during the year and is actively aware of the decisions or recommendations of the planning committee, the plans and strengths of the finance committee, and those of the fund raising committee. Considering where the institution is in its present development, and the direction in which the institution should head, the nominating committee then identifies quite specifically what particular talents or areas of expertise are necessary to have on the board in order to assist in moving the institution more directly toward where it wants to go. If the board as a whole has not already done so, the nominating committee also should insist that a resolution be passed stating clearly what is expected, on at least a minimal basis, of all board members. The nominating committee should then review the present membership of the board, determining how many of the identified human needs are being satisfied or filled by the present trustees and what gaps exist that need filling. The committee also should review the commitment of present board members in terms of the criteria for membership resolution approved by the board. *When the particular needs have been identified, and only then, is it time to begin to discuss specific names of possible new board members.*

It may be that no one on the nominating committee knows individuals who might be qualified to fill the identified institutional needs. In that case, and if such knowledge is not available from the rest of the board or staff, it is the responsibility of the committee to determine how to find out who such persons might be. In this case, it will likely be necessary to seek advice from appropriate persons in the community. Even if a committee member does not know a person from whom he or she wishes to obtain advice, it is quite simple to arrange an appointment to seek advice if he or she is up front in regard to the purpose of the appointment. Most people are not only willing to give advice but are actually flattered to be asked.

After identifying the individuals who it is felt would make good trustees, the committee should report to the full board, seeking further comment and obtaining the board's permission to sound out the possible candidates for trusteeship as to their real interests, availability, and potential commitment. It should also be decided who is the best, or are the best, members of the board and staff to discuss potential trusteeship with the individual. Depending on the institution's structure, it normally is a very good idea to have either the artistic director or top management person present at the meeting where a potential board member is being recruited. If a board member knows the prospective member, he or she also is a likely person to do the recruiting. If no one knows the individual reasonably well, then it is the responsibility of the board president, board chairman, or nominating committee chairman to make the appointment and lead the discussion, again with the artistic or management leader accompanying him or her. During the course of the conversation with the potential trustee, it should be made clear exactly what is expected in terms of time, effort, and money. This may well frighten a potential trustee away, but it is much better to know in advance that the individual will not, or can not, do what is expected.

Recently, an institution that was moving into a new stage of development and wished to strengthen its board in a variety of ways and also wished to attract some of the more prominent citizens of the community to the board, gambled on being up front in its recruitment. It formed a list of people, seven of whom would be finally elected to board membership. In the interview process, and particularly when the specific criteria for board membership were stated, four of the so-called prime potential board members refused. Two of them turned down the idea of trusteeship completely. Two of them requested that they be reconsidered for board membership the following year as their current commitments precluded accepting the new responsibilities as outlined. As a result of the process, the board ended up with seven new members who at least verbalized their commitment to fulfill what they were told was expected of them. Although nervous initially about the process, the members of the nominating committee at the end were emphatic in their satisfaction that they had not brought individuals on to the board who could not truly serve the needs of the institution. They also reported that those interviewed about potential board membership indicated their appreciation of the candor.

When individuals are interviewed initially as potential board members, the impression must not be given that they are being formally invited to join the board. In fact, the board has not yet elected them. Based on the outcome of the interviews, the nominating committee should then prepare a slate for election by the full board.

Who Elects Board Members   The power to elect board members normally is specified in the by-laws of the institution. Basically, in a corporate sense, there are two types of not-for-profit professional performing arts institutions: 1. membership corporations and 2. non-membership corporations.

In most not-for-profit professional performing arts membership corporations, the power to elect trustees lies with the members. *Historically, most such membership institutions established membership* (with members' rights specified in the by-laws) *for fund raising, not legal, reasons.* With the contribution of "x" dollars, usually rather low, an individual in the community could become a member. In return for the contribution, he or she would be invited to the annual meeting of the membership and perhaps receive some other benefits, e.g., first choice of seats, special parking arrangements, a newsletter, a hot-line to the box office. In membership corporations, the primary item of business at the annual membership meeting is to elect the trustees of the institution. Different membership corporations have established different quorums of the total membership necessary to make the annual meeting a legally constituted meeting. The percentage of members necessary for a quorum normally is not very large; thus, during the course of an institution's history, it is perfectly possible, if and when differences of opinion evolve, that a relatively small group of determined members can throw out a board of trustees and replace it with one that reflects the then current dissident view. As a part of such a coup, it also is possible to get rid of the artistic director and/or top management. Usually it is the responsibility of the board of trustees to hire and fire those two or three leaders.

This manual urges any institution that is based legally on membership to reassess its position and act to change it. Confusion of fund raising needs with legal structure is potentially dangerous to the integrity of the institution. The right to vote for election of members of the board of trustees should not be based on the contribution of dollars to support the artistic program of the institution. In those states requiring that not-for-profit institutions be membership corporations, there is a very simple answer which is totally within the law. In such cases, the by-laws would state that the board of trustees of the institution constitutes the membership of the corporation.

One ballet company has a unique variation on the legal membership structure. The members of that corporation elect the board of trustees. The members themselves, however, are elected to membership by a small group of what are termed life members. These life members are elected for life by other life members, including the original founding members. Although a percentage of life members is necessary to establish a quorum for the conduct of a meeting of the life membership, in the event a quorum is not present, any life member can still hold a valid meeting of life members. What this really means is that if any very small number of life members decided to do so, they probably could get away with completely changing the balance of the membership and of the institution itself, through the membership's election of the board.

In non-membership corporations, or in membership corporations where the board of trustees, as a body, is designated as the membership of the corporation, *the board of trustees normally is elected by the board members then serving in office at the time of the election.* Trustee election usually takes place at the annual meeting of the board. Candidates for election are normally those nominated by the nominating committee. A majority vote of those present at a meeting where a quorum is present normally is necessary to elect an individual to the board. By-laws should include a provision enabling election of trustees at meetings other than the annual meeting, e.g., at any regular meeting of the board or at a special meeting called for that purpose.

While some argue that the election of trustees by existing trustees cannot help but be incestuous or cloning, a board that takes its responsibilities seriously and uses its nominating committee wisely and efficiently, can preclude such from happening.

Board Orientation   The following contribution was written by Ann S. Smith, former Trustee of the Cleveland Ballet.

BOARD ORIENTATION
by Ann S. Smith

The process of board orientation and development begins before the selection of a single board member and continues throughout the life of an organization. A successful, effective orientation program insures that each person who serves on the board is used to his or her fullest potential and that the board, as a legal entity, fulfills its fiduciary obligations to the organization.

Basic elements of any orientation program provide prospective or active board members with the information, direction, and motivation to do their job well. These elements include a knowledge of the organization – its purposes, its goals, its plans for the future. They also should include an exploration in sufficient detail of the artistic goals, administrative goals, and financial status of the company, In addition to providing a long-range view, this information helps the new trustees place themselves in the organization.

The board plays a vital role of equal importance to that of artistic and administrative staff of the organization. Careful planning should go into preparing the board for this role. The entire process should be tailored to the organization. The age of the organization, its artistic purposes, its role in the community, and the current strength of its operations should all be taken into account. A thorough analysis of the existing board – its size, terms, available skills, financial strength, and overall commitment – identifies target areas for adding new members and for reorienting existing ones to broaden the potential of the organization. The extent to which the executive staff, appropriate board chairs, and artistic directors have researched the existing situation is critical. Each part of this management team must have a comprehensive understanding of the current situation before making decisions about board orientation.

The activities of board orientation can be viewed as two interrelated functions: 1. the selection and education of new board members and 2. the evaluation, motivation, and redirection of existing trustees.

Neither activity actually precedes the other. In the organization's annual business cycle, there should be both a fixed time for the routine functions of each process and flexibility to adjust or add to the process if board members must be replaced midyear or if other unforseen contingencies arise.

Let us first look at the orientation of new members. Whether they are being called together as the first board of trustees, to expand an existing board, or to replace members lost through planned or unplanned attrition, each new person has been chosen on the basis of the skills he/she brings to the organization, the financial resources he/she can provide or lead to and his/her particular suitability to the job at hand. You know these reasons, your management team knows these reasons – make sure from the beginning that the new trustee knows them as well. Discuss your expectations clearly and honestly from the start; it will help avoid future misunderstandings and help you identify the potential of each new member.

If trustees are expected to meet their responsibilities, the management team must be willing and prepared to fulfill its commitment to its responsibilities well. Managers must be thoroughly prepared to make decisions and schedules with appropriate notice, to hold to those schedules for trustee activities, and to provide thorough, well-written and designed materials for the trustees' information. In essence, management and the trustees will be entering into an agreement in principle to work responsibly for the organization.

The following table gives examples of the responsibilities expected of each party to this agreement. These responsibilities should be clearly explained to the new member before appointment to the board:

Expected Trustee Performance	*Management Actions Required*
a) Annual financial donation	Set minimum donation amount. Collect contribution before first meeting of fiscal year.
b) Meeting attendance	Provide annual schedule of board meetings, committee meetings, and special functions. Indicate meeting purposes and which ones are considered mandatory.
c) Advice on financial operations	Present sufficiently detailed financial reports and projections prior to board appointment and at all subsequent board meetings. Be frank about the organization's financial prospectus.
d) Contribution solicitation	Interview prospective board member and make sure he or she knows this responsibility. With fund raising chair, staff, and new trustee, draft a list of projected target donors or goods or services.
e) Ticket purchase	Set aside sufficient prime seats and make them available for purchase prior to general sales.
f) Advice on projects	Provide sufficient historical background, clear purpose statements, and detailed information on organization's philosophies and resources.

g) Committee service	Place new trustee on one or more committees before election. Discuss new trustee's interests and organization's needs in selecting appropriate Committee assignment.

The newly acquired trustee should be immersed in the operation and social life of the organization as quickly as possible. Take care, however, to avoid overwhelming them or overtaxing their time. One effective method uses a series of three well-focused meetings.

First, the trustee meets with the chief executive of the organization, chairman of the committee on trustees (a must for every board)*, the board president, and the artistic director of the organization. At this session, the trustee is given a general background and briefing of the organization's history, directions, and needs. Next the trustee is given a tour of the facilities during rehearsal activity to get a feel for the artistic process at work and to catch the spirit of the organization as a whole. Finally, the trustee attends a social gathering for new members hosted by management and the committee on trustees. New members meet one another and raise questions that may remain among them before actual board service begins. While these three activities can be combined and need not be time-consuming affairs, all three aspects should be properly addressed. If each aspect has been effectively presented and sufficient time has been spent in preparation, the new trustee will enter his or her term with a solid understanding and appreciation of the business function, the philosophy, and the interpersonal political life of the organization.

Periodic orientation of trustees mid-term is often necessary and always beneficial. The management team should work closely with the board president and committee on trustees to monitor the performance of board members relative to the changing conditions of the organization. At a minimum, the president should personally contact each member twice a year. The president's call can simply address the trustees' questions and concerns that may have been overlooked in the regular course of business. A strong, trusting relationship with board members can often reveal potential problems and useful ideas that would otherwise have gone unnoticed. Moreover, the whole issue of trustee motivation and morale plays an important role in the effectiveness of the board.

Major reorientation may be required because of significant organization changes, unusually high attrition, or simply because the current board structure is ineffective. In the first case, a process similar to the original orientation may prove effective if you take into account the level of understanding already achieved. Since the board itself would have been involved in the organization's restructure, they will be

*(Note: FEDAPT recommends that the role of the committee on trustees be assumed by the nominating committee.)

able to provide guidance on the amount of reorientation required. High attrition or a poorly functioning board usually indicates severe problems in the organization as a whole. An intensive internal review is in order. Outside help may be required as well. In any case, until the root cause has been identified and corrected, board reorientation would be of little value.

A common problem among arts organizations is the desire of the board to become involved in artistic decisions for the company. By being clear about the limits of board authority and by bringing together the trustees and artistic staff during the orientation period, this problem can usually be avoided.

Board orientation can be a creative and productive process. Tailoring orientation materials and group processes to the specific conditions of the organization requires a flexible interpretation of these guidelines and a tough look at the organization's resources.

Depending on the size and complexity of board operations, a simple attractively designed board manual of a few pages, or a more complex and expensive set of orientation materials, meetings, and audio visual presentations, may be chosen. But whatever the extent of the operations, if crucial information is clearly, concisely presented, and board responsibilities and authority are taken seriously, the potential of each individual will be realized. The reward will be a highly motivated, skilled group of advisers that can greatly extend the organization's management and financial capabilities.

Ann Sheridan Smith

Ann Sheridan Smith is the Director of Development for the National Opera Institute which assists and encourages the artists and institutions of American Opera/Musical Theatre. Ms. Smith is the Co-Chairman of the Dance Advisory Panel of the National Endowment for the Arts and has served as a grants panelist for the Ohio Arts Council. She was Vice President and a founding member of the Cleveland Ballet where she acted as liaison between board and staff and authored the board development plan. Prior to this she pursued a career in sales and hotel management. Ms. Smith has been a board member of Ohio Citizens Committee for the Arts and the Association of Ohio Dance Companies.

Terms of Office for Board Members   The way most by-laws of not-for-profit professional performing arts institutions are written, there is no provision to rotate trustees off boards after a fixed period of time. In many cases, the by-laws specify that a trustee is elected to serve for a specific number of years per term, e.g., for one, two, or three years. *Normally, however, no limit is placed on the number of consecutive terms a trustee may serve. Without such limitation, trustees may serve indefinitely if they wish. It often is very difficult to get rid of a trustee who wishes to remain on a board but who is not an active or productive trustee, because of this non-limitation on* *length of service.*

When institutions are founded and new boards are recruited, there rarely is any thought given to future implications of not having a rotation-off provision in the by-laws. Usually, those creating a board are so delighted at finding people who are willing to serve, they can't conceive the problem of having to get rid of a trustee who should not be on the board. Perhaps more important, however, than the question of getting rid of unproductive trustees in a graceful way, is how best to provide for bringing new blood into the institution. No matter how good a trustee an individual is perceived to be, most humans who provide active, dedicated service begin to tire after a certain period of time. Also, it is natural for people to feel they are doing a reasonably good job after a period of time and to feel that, based on their experience, they pretty well know what is good for the institution. The result often is the development of at least some degree of inflexibility.

Two consecutive three-year terms, or three consecutive two-year terms, should be the maximum number of years a trustee should serve without a break. If three-year terms are decided on, the total number of elected trustees on the board should be divisible by three. The board should be divided into three classes so that the three-year terms of one-third of the board terminate each year. If two-year terms are prescribed, the total number of elected trustees serving on the board should be divisible by two. The board should be divided into two classes, with the two-year terms of one-half the board terminating each year. This does not mean that one-third or one-half of the board actually will be replaced each year, as it is more than likely that a number of trustees will be reelected to a second or third term. *However, the rotation-off policy will provide for the introduction on a regular basis of new individuals, and presumably new thinking, to the board.*

Such delineation of terms and the establishment of a rotation-off policy should result in a stronger, more effective nominating committee. Not only will the nominating committee be responsible for a review of board members' service according to the criteria of board membership established by board resolution as discussed above, but based on that review the nominating committee should determine whether or not a trustee should be reelected for a second three-year term or a second or third two-year term. Just because a limit is placed on the number of consecutive terms a trustee may serve, it does not mean that each trustee should be reelected to serve the maximum allowable consecutive terms. *An individual should be nominated for reelection only if he or she has at least lived up to the minimum criteria of service as established by the board.* This provision for limitation on years of service can also work to the advantage of the institution in another way. A person being recruited to a board may well feel more willing to serve if he or she knows there is a limit on the number of years of service expected. It also allows a trustee to choose not to be reelected and to leave the board gracefully at the end of either a two- or a three-year term.

An argument frequently made against the establishment of a rotation-off policy is that the institution would then lose the service of valuable trustees who otherwise would be willing to continue to serve but who are precluded from doing so when the specified consecutive terms of service are completed. It is not necesary to lose such an individual. The trustees may be reelected to another series of terms following the lapse of one year after completion of the first series of consecutive terms. Further, if provision is made in the by-laws for service by non-board members on board committees, the individual who has been rotated off for a year, may serve actively on a board committee during the year before reelection to the board. This provision will be discussed below in the section on standing and ad hoc committees.

Board Officers and Terms of Office   Technically, the officers of the board are the officers of the corporation. Normally, the by-laws of not-for-profit professional performing arts institutions provide for at least the following: president, vice president, treasurer, and secretary. Some by-laws also provide for assistant vice presidents, treasurers, and secretaries. When the word "should" or "shall" is used in by-laws, it means that such *must* be done. If the word "may" is used, it means it is *permissable* or *allowable* to do so. Some by-laws provide that one person may hold more than one of the four principal officer positions at the same time unless the law prohibits it. Normally, however, if the board is a working board and if the trustees are active in support of the institution, *it is better to have the principal officer positions filled by four different individuals*. For effective functioning of the board, particularly in regard to taking and distributing minutes of meetings, it may be of value to provide that the secretary *not* be a member of the board.

Trustees are usually elected to board membership at the annual meeting of the board. This often is followed immediately by the election of officers. Officers may be elected to serve terms of any length, but the usual term is for one year. Many boards, however, do not have any limit on the number of consecutive one-year terms an officer may serve in any particular office. As in the case of board membership tenure, *a rotation-off policy should be established for officers. It is recommended that an individual should not be permitted to serve in one office for more than three consecutive one-year terms.* A provision such as this does not mean that an incumbent will or should continue to serve in office for the maximum permissable period of time. One-year terms of office provide the opportunity to change officers each year if that proves necessary for the good of the institution, but the provision for up to three years in an office permits continuity of service for an effective, dedicated board officer. The exception to a limited term of years in office should be provided for in the case of secretary. If the office of the secretary is, for example, held by a staff person who is not a member of the board, and while the secretary should be elected each year, it should be possible for that person to continue to act as secretary for as long as the board feels he or she is performing the duties of that office effectively.

Some institutions also include the office of chairman in addition to that of president. Sometimes this is done for fund raising or quasi-public relations reasons and the chairmanship is more or less an honorific position. In such an instance, the chairman often is designated as the individual to chair the annual meeting, while the president chairs the other regular meetings of the board. In other instances, where the title of president is accorded the top salaried executive of the institution (e.g., some presidents of symphony orchestras or presenting institutions), the chairman of the board fills the same function as the president of a board where the presidential title is not used for a senior staff person.

In some institutions, staff persons are accorded corporate officer titles (other than secretary) but are not board members. In at least one major theatre, the artistic director and the managing director are officers of the corporation but are not members of the board of trustees. In another not-for-profit professional performing arts institution that also is a presenting institution, the president of the institution is the top salaried person in charge of the overall operation of the institution and also serves as a full member of the board and is president of the board, under the chairman of the board.

Whenever possible, the officer structure should be kept simple and the purpose of the office described clearly and succinctly.

There is no right or wrong in regard to staff members serving as members of the board of trustees. Arguments can be advanced supporting either point of view. It really depends on what type of institution it is and what the reasons are for or against such service. It is not unusual to find that an artistic director who has created the institution of which he or she is artistic leader, also serves as a full voting member of the board. It is less usual to find managing directors serving as board members. It is not common to find artistic directors as board members of institutions they did not found. One theatre company includes on its board up to four members of the artistic and management staffs in addition to the artistic and managing directors. This board feels strongly that the input received from working staff is vital to the decision-making process and also believes that the rest of the company feels more a part of the total institution because of the feedback provided them by their peers. These staff members serving on the board are not considered to be, nor do they act as, representatives of the staff, protecting staff rights. Rather, they act as members of the board of the total institution, with a particular expertise as artists, technicians, or administrators in much the same way an accountant or a lawyer brings his or her professional expertise to the board as a whole.

Whatever decision any institution reaches in regard to members of staff serving on a board should be made consciously in terms of what is best for that particular institution, not on the basis of a theory or formula that advocates either staff or non-staff participation on the board.

Whether or not staff members serve as members of the board, *no meeting of the board or any of its committees should take place without an appropriate staff member present.* As will be discussed later, each board committee should have some form of staff support. The individual responsible for providing that support should attend all meetings of that committee. Board meetings should, with very rare, if any, exceptions be attended by either the artistic leader or the top management leader, preferably both. An exception might be when the board wishes to go into executive session to discuss the salaries of the top artistic and management leaders, or when the question of the dismissal of either is under consideration. Normally, however, those two or three individuals should be present or should expect to be present at board meetings.

The board of a not-for-profit professional performing arts institution is not in existence as an end in and of itself. It is a part of the total institutional team which presumably is dedicated to the definition and implementation of the artistic purpose of the institution. As such, it is vital for the artistic and management leadership to be present and participate in all discussions dealing with such definition and implementation. Due to such demands on time as rehearsal and production, it may not always be possible for the artistic director to attend all board meetings, but it must be assumed that in his or her absence, the managing director is able to speak from the perspective of both the artistic and management leadership.

Standing and Ad Hoc Committees In an earlier section of this manual, a recommendation for the provision for both standing and ad hoc committees of the board was made and the purposes of some were described. *The by-laws of the institution should provide not only for the existence of board committees, but also for the manner in which they are established.* There should be an indication of how individuals become committee members, what is the tenure of committee membership, and what constitutes a quorum for a committee meeting. The president or chairman of the board normally appoints the chairman of any standing and ad hoc committees and also serves as an ex officio voting member of each committee. An exception to this should be appointment of the chairman of the nominating committee. This position is increasingly being filled as a result of the affirmative vote of a majority of the board. The basic reason for this is to preclude the possibility, unlikely though it may seem, of any board president or chairman exercising any potentially undue influence on the composition of the board or on the selection of the officers. Such is not usually a problem but there is the example of one board president who named himself chairman of the nominating committee and who, because there was no rotation-off policy, had served, when last heard about, for more than twenty years. Over the course of years, he managed to get people elected to the board who would support what he wanted, including his own appointment as salaried managing director of the institution, while continuing to serve as president of the board. This is, of course, a most unusual case, but it does demonstrate a possibility.

The treasurer of the board frequently serves as chairman of the finance committee. This may be a logical combination of offices in the same individual who presumably has the professional experience to satisfy the requirements of the dual responsibility. Depending on the situation and needs of the institution, it may well be more productive to divide these responsibilities between two individuals.

Committee members and committee chairman should be appointed to serve one-year renewable terms. In contrast to tenure as board members or as officers, there is no reason to limit the number of one-year terms a committee member may serve, with the exception of the nominating committee. *The chairman and members of the nominating committee should probably not serve more than three consecutive one-year terms.* Further, the dates of tenure of members of this committee should be staggered, so that there is continuity provided when some of the members rotate on and off each year. Committee appointments normally should be made at the annual meeting of the board, but the board may approve establishment of additional standing and ad hoc committees at any meeting of the board; and the president or chairman of the board may appoint members at any time as vacancies occur or following the creation of new board-appointed committees.

The section of the by-laws providing for committees should provide for the possibility of appointing non-board members as full voting members of board committees. With this provision, it is possible to retain the active services of a board member who must be rotated off the board for at least a year before reelection. It is also possible to assure continued service of a valuable board member who is rotating off the board and who does not wish to be considered for reelection to the board, but who is willing to serve actively on a committee for the good of the institution. This provision can serve as a good recruiting mechanism. Potential board members can be tested through service on a committee before making the fuller commitment as a board member. It also can be used as a way of attracting particular individuals with special abilities to serve the institution without making the commitments that accompany full board membership. An example of the latter is in the area of fund raising. There might well be an individual in the community who would be willing to devote a limited amount of time to assisting in the general fund raising effort or special benefits effort, but who is not able or willing to commit the time necessary to full board membership. As a voting member of the fund raising committee, he or she is a full member of a defined or delineated activity and has the sense of responsible participation as a voting committee member.

The one exception to having non-board members as voting members of board committees is the executive committee. Because the executive committee usually is empowered to act on behalf of the board between meetings of the board, non-board members should not be given such authority. If an executive committee exists, it should include in its membership at least the officers of the board. Further, to be effective, it is appropriate to include the chairmen of all the standing committees. This does not necessarily mean that the executive committee will be a large one. A number of the committee chairs may be held by officers, e.g., finance committee chairmanship held by the treasurer.

Minutes of committee meetings should be kept and, if desired, distributed to all members of the board. *The minutes of the executive committee meetings should be distributed to all members of the board as soon as possible after the committee meets.* The need for this action has been discussed in an earlier section of this manual. The minutes of each committee meeting should probably be written by the staff member serving in a support capacity to the committee and should be reviewed with the chairman of the committee before distribution.

Each board committee should have a member of the staff assigned to it. An obvious example of the rationale of this is the assignment of the development director, or fund raising director, to the fund raising committee. It is this individual or his or her office that keeps the detailed records on giving and which plans and implements, with committee assistance and input, the fund raising activities of the institution. The managing director, or perhaps the business manager of a large-staff institution, works with the finance committee. Both the artistic director and the managing director (or top management person irrespective of title) should work with the executive, nominating, and planning committees. If both cannot attend, it is important that at least one do so.

Committees should meet only if there is a purpose in doing so. Based on the purpose and function of the committee, an estimate can be made of the number of regular committee meetings necessary during each year. The dates of those meetings should be scheduled on an annual basis. Other meetings may be convened as necessary, but only if necessary. With this type of scheduling, each committee member will know the time involvement estimated and normally will be able to work it into his or her schedule. The agendas for committee meetings should be worked out in advance of the meeting by the staff person serving in a support role to the committee, in conjunction with the committee chairman. Each meeting should be scheduled for only the period of time necessary to accomplish the purpose of the meeting. If meetings start on time and if they end on time, committee members are more likely to arrive on time and can schedule themselves to remain through the meeting. If as is too often the case, a meeting drags on beyond what is thought to have been the time for closing, members may get in the habit of leaving early. With specified times established, a member is free to make appointments for before and after the meeting with confidence in being able to fulfill all obligations. *The agenda for a regular meeting of a committee should be sent to all members of the committee as part of the reminder notice of the meeting.* Not only is sharing an agenda with committee members in advance of the meeting a courtesy, it also enables the members to give some thought to the content of the meeting beforehand. If possible, any pertinent materials also should be sent out in advance.

The following contribution on board committees has been written by Tony H. Dechario, General Manager of the Rochester (New York) Philharmonic Orchestra.

BOARD COMMITTEES
by Tony H. Dechario

In examining the criteria for effective committee structure in a not-for-profit arts organization, it might be helpful to first review the relationship of committees to the overall organizational structure. The key body in a not-for-profit organization is, of course, the board of trustees. The board, in conjunction with the artistic and management leadership of the organization, works toward: 1. establishing the goals (objectives) of the organization (generally outlined in the organizational charter); 2. creating programs to achieve those goals; 3. setting policy for implementing the programs; 4. providing for the financial needs of the organization so that the programs can be implemented.

In order to fulfill these responsibilities, most boards find it useful to establish working committees from their memberships to: 1. study issues and alternative avenues of action; 2. recommend specific action to the full board; 3. carry out programs adopted by the board (although the latter may be directed in part or wholly to the staff, depending upon the size of the staff in relationship to the task). Some committees may from time to time be given the authority by the full board to take action in specific areas.

Organizations may choose to establish committees in a variety of ways. Small organizations may wish to limit the number of committees to two or three, while larger organizations may wish to establish as many as ten to twelve committees. It may be helpful to define certain general avenues of traditional committee responsibility and explore an organization's options in dividing that responsibility among committees.

Committee functions can be divided between those that are ongoing and those that are short-term. The former class should be assigned to standing committees; that is committees remaining in place from year to year, even though their membership and, in fact, the membership of the board may change. Standing committees should be established to address three major functional areas: 1. the executive function; 2. the financial function; 3. program and planning functions.

The Executive Function

The *executive committee* is the primary committee in this area. The executive committee assists the president in carrying out his or her responsibilities and often acts in lieu of the board between meetings. When emergency situations arise and a full board meeting cannot be called (except in regard to issues specifically reserved for the board or full membership by the by-laws). This committee should be composed entirely of board members and primarily of officers of the organization. Some organizations may wish to establish a separate *personnel committee* to address staff policies and act as a performance review committee for senior staff.

The Financial Function

Smaller organizations may wish to have the executive committee function as the *finance committee*. Most organizations, however, will want a separate committee to handle this function. The finance committee is charged with adopting an operating budget, reviewing the financial posture of the organization on a periodic basis (generally monthly or quarterly), and providing for adequate accounting and cash management practices. Membership in this committee should include persons whose expertise falls in the financial area (such as accountants, bankers, businessmen) who also have an understanding of and commitment to the organization's mission. Larger organizations may want to establish subcommittees of the finance committee or separate committees with responsibility in areas such as *investment management, audit, pension management, and insurance.*

The Program and Planning Function

Smaller organizations with one or two separate programs may wish to have a single *program committee* composed of persons who have specific knowledge and/or expertise in the program areas. Larger organizations may need separate committees in areas such as *artistic policy, marketing, subscription sales, fund raising,* and *public affairs.* Public (government) affairs obviously requires persons with contacts to public officials.

Within the overall program area, a *long-range planning* function should be an ongoing committee responsibility. The long-range planning activity requires participation from persons representing a cross-section of board interest (finance, program, and executive) as well as principal artistic and management staff. Some issues relate to specific short-term goals or needs. Ad hoc committees may be needed to address those specific issues or needs, even though they are issues that fall under the purview of a standing committee.

Within the personnel area, a *search committee* to fill a senior artistic or management staff position is often established as the need arises. A *negotiating committee* can be established to negotiate a specific labor agreement or specific contract with another organization. A *nominating committee* to recommend new board members and/or officers of the board is usually provided for in the organization's by-laws and can be either a standing or ad hoc committee. In addition, ad hoc committees are often formed to deal with specific programs (e.g., pension fund concerts, special exhibitions, etc.).

A committee generally reports to the full board through its chairman, relating programs in its area of responsibility or recommending specific action. Where an organization has several committees, it can be helpful to have vice presidents with responsibility for specific committees to coordinate the flow of information to and from the board.

Committee membership need not be limited to board members. Membership on committees provides an organization with the opportunity to take advantage of the interest and experience of non-board members in the community and is an excellent training ground for future board members.

Finally, many organizations establish auxiliary organizations that relate to the parent organization as a "committee of the board." Women's committees, junior boards, and committees representing the organization's interests in different geographical areas can effectively report to and recommend action to the organization's board through the same process as the board's own committees.

Tony H. Dechario

Tony H. Dechario has served as General Manager of the Rochester Philharmonic Orchestra (Rochester, NY) since 1975. He had been second trombone of the RPO since 1965, and since 1972 had also served as Personnel Manager. A graduate of the Eastman School of Music, Mr. Dechario played with the Kansas City Philharmonic and the Dallas Symphony before joining the RPO.

Advisory, Honorary, and Emeritus Groups Many institutions have established advisory boards, advisory committees, honorary boards, emeritus boards, or ex officio board memberships for a wide variety of reasons. Most have been done for direct or indirect fund raising, public relations, or political purposes. Anything can be done if provided for in or not prohibited by the by-laws. If any such special groups of individual positions are formed, it should be done with a very clear purpose in mind, and *the individuals invited to accept such positions should understand why they are being invited.* The most misunderstood and misused (or not used) group is the so-called advisory board or advisory committee. Assumed in the name is the need of, and desire for, advice from individuals qualified in some way to provide it. In reality, however, most advisory committees or advisory boards are window dressing with names of members usually being recognized names in a community, thus implying the granting of a seal of approval to the institution. *If the advice of a group is not really desired, the group should have some other title such as honorary support committee or the like. In no case should the word "board" be associated with an honorary or advisory support group.* This frequently leads to confusion. There is only one board for each not-for-profit professional performing arts institution. It should remain the only body accorded use of the word *board.*

An institution may decide that for any of a variety of reasons it wishes to single out a particular individual for special recognition. If such recognition cannot really be given through the establishment of some sort of honorary group, there is no reason that the by-laws of the institution cannot provide for honorary ex officio board positions, e.g., emeritus trustees or honorary trustees. All individuals who have served on the board would not become emeritus trustees in such a case. Rather, the positions should be reserved for board members who have served the institution in an especially outstanding manner. Honorary trustees might be the designation for those in the community who have been, or who could be, of outstanding service, although not members of the board. Some institutions choose to name certain public officials as honorary trustees, or simply, as ex officio trustees, i.e., trustees because of the office they hold, not the individual persons they are. If such ex officio positions are provided for in the by-laws, it should be clear whether or not they have a vote on the board. It is not enough to state that a position is ex officio. There are voting ex officio positions as well as ex officio positions without vote. *Each time the title ex officio is used, it should be qualified in regard to vote.* Normally, ex officio positions without vote do not count in terms of determining whether or not a quorum is present for a meeting. Again, this should be specified.

Committee reports as well as committee recommendations for action by the board should be reported to the board by the chairman of the committees. Some boards are structured so that the executive committee screens everything coming from another committee of the board before it is presented to the full board. Normally, however, it is not necessary, nor within policy, to refer committee recommendations to the executive committee for approval prior to submission to the full board. In the case of a particularly large board, where the executive committee may act or tends to act as a "normal" board, committee recommendations usually are referred to the executive committee for action or recommendation for action prior to submission to the board. Some potential problems that can arise when an institution has a strong executive committee have been discussed earlier in this manual.

Quorums and Proxies Unless counter to state law, each institution may establish its own provisions governing the use of proxies and the establishment of quorums necessary for legitimate meetings. The decisions on these topics should be included in the by-laws.

The number constituting a quorum for a meeting of a board of trustees normally is a majority of the trustees then serving in office. It is, however, important to be specific. If, for example, the by-laws provide for a specific number of trustees, say twenty-seven, a majority of the number of trustees necessary to establish a quorum for a meeting would be fourteen. However, there may be vacancies on the board and there may be only twenty-one trustees actually in office. This should result in requiring the presence of eleven trustees to constitute a quorum. However, unless the provision for a quorum specifically refers to "x" number or percent of trustees *then serving in office,* it could be argued that the quorum must be fourteen, not eleven.

Each institution should give careful thought to what its quorum requirements should be. The quorum figure should be low enough to assure that the legal business of the institution can be taken care of, but high enough so it is the responsibility of board members to make every effort to attend meetings and so that a small group cannot take over the institution. *Unless there is a compelling reason to provide differently, a quorum should not be less than a majority of those trustees then serving in office.* If only less than a majority of board members are willing and able to attend at least the regular meetings of the board, there is something very wrong with the structure or morale of the institution and/or choice of board members which has been made. If one of the criteria of board membership is attendance at board meetings, if board meetings are not boring, if boards are not constantly coping with real or perceived crisis situations, if board meetings are scheduled well in advance, if board meetings begin and end when they are supposed to, and if the executive committee is not acting too much and too often on behalf of the board, there is every likelihood that a majority of the trustees will attend and the attaining of a quorum will not be a problem.

To pass a motion normally requires an affirmative vote of a majority of board members attending in person a meeting at which a quorum is present. Consideration should be given, however, to two exceptions to this rule. *It is recommended that a two-thirds vote of the total board members then serving in office be required for the amendment of by-laws as well as for the removal of any member of the board or officer of the corporation.* Again using a twenty-seven member board as an example, if any motion is passed by the affirmative vote of a majority of those present at a meeting at which there is a quorum, eight trustees could amend the by-laws or remove a board member or officer. (Fourteen members would constitute a quorum. Eight members would be the majority of those at a meeting at which the minimum for a quorum were in attendance). Establishing a rule requiring an affirmative vote of two-thirds of all trustees serving in office would necessitate a total of eighteen votes (rather than eight) to amend by-laws or remove trustees or officers.

With a board of fifteen, the comparative figures would be five and ten.

Quorums also should be established for the conduct of meetings of board committees. A simple majority of the committee members then serving in office normally constitutes a quorum.

The by-laws of some not-for-profit professional performing arts institutions provide for the use of proxies. *This manual recommends strongly that no institution entertain the right of proxy voting on any matter.* In the case of the for-profit corporation, proxies are vital to the existence of the corporation. Boards of directors of such corporations are elected by the shareholders. It is understood and accepted that there is no practical or possible way to get all the shareholders, or even a majority of shareholders, of a publicly held for-profit corporation together at a meeting for the election of directors. Proxies are, therefore, solicited by management to enable the formality of elections to take place. The same is true for other items of business that come before the shareholders at the annual meeting of the for-profit corporation.

For the not-for-profit corporation, there is absolutely no similar need. If the corporation is based on membership (a concept strongly recommended against in this manual), it should be the responsibility of the members to vote in person. Many membership corporations get around this problem, if they do not provide for proxies, by establishing a quorum for the annual meeting of the membership which is small enough to assure legality of the meeting. For the not-for-profit institution that has no members, or the board of trustees that constitutes the membership, no proxy voting should be allowed. If the board of trustees is in fact an integral part of the institutional team, if the individual trustees know clearly what is expected of them as board members, and if the trustees understand fully their responsibilities, obligations, and privileges of service, there is no room, need, or legitimacy to voting by proxy.

Board Meetings *The by-laws of the institutions should provide for the holding of annual, regular, and special meetings of the board.* The by-laws need not state specifically how often the board should meet. That detail should be covered by board resolution each year and should be determined by the real needs of the institution. At certain times in an institution's development, it may be valuable to have regular monthly meetings of the board. At another point, however, meetings every other month or quarterly, or on another pattern, might be more appropriate.

The annual meeting of the board should be set for a time that is most beneficial to the institution. For example, the annual meeting should not be held in conjunction with the need for a vote on an important and/or possibly complex item of board business such as the budget. No new trustee, assuming he or she is elected and takes office at the annual meeting, or assumes office at the board meeting immediately following the annual meeting, should be expected to vote at that time on the annual budget of the institution. *Thus, the annual meeting should be held subsequent to the meeting that approves the budget for the fiscal year.* Because such budget approval always should occur prior to the start of the fiscal year for which the budget has been prepared, it may in fact not be possible to schedule the annual meeting until after the fiscal year has started. This is no problem. If one of the purposes of the annual meeting is to elect trustees and officers and to appoint committee members, the date of the meeting should be set for when it is to the greatest advantage of the institution to have these decisions made.

Special meetings of the board should only be called when absolutely necessary and for a special purpose. If staff and board members agree that special meetings are to be very few, if any, in number, then matters that might otherwise be considered as special, will and can be dealt with in regularly scheduled meetings.

There is no day of the week or time of the day that is particularly good for board meetings. Frequency of meetings during the year should be decided after careful discussion of the institution's needs among board and staff. Based on the decision of frequency, specific days and months should be decided upon by the board and staff, taking into account the artistic and management professional schedules as well as the professional and personal obligations of the members of the board. *The important thing is to establish firm dates well in advance (normally at the annual meeting) for regularly scheduled meetings* so that all will know and get the dates on their calendars. Reminder notices should, of course, be sent out by the staff.

The time of day for regular board meetings is another point that must be decided upon in advance and adhered to. There is no one time that is better than another. Different communities have different perceptions about when the best time is for boards (volunteers) to meet. Whatever is agreeable to the largest number of board members is what should be decided upon. As was mentioned in connection with scheduling committee meetings, *it is important that meeting of the board have both a scheduled time to begin and a scheduled time to end.* With rare exception, these times should be adhered to strictly. In general, less business is achieved effectively at a board meeting that takes place while a meal is being eaten. It is difficult to concentrate on a particular problem or point of discussion if one's mind really is concerned with getting the salt shaker or the cream for the coffee.

The site of the meeting is another decision not to be taken lightly. There is a tendency, particularly in urban areas, for board meetings to take place in the office facilities of one of the board members, or at a conveniently located club or other such facility. Board meetings held in private homes frequently turn into social occasions rather than being work sessions. This is all right on occasion, but if at all possible, *most board meetings should take place at the facility of which the board members are trustees.* They are a part of that institution and need to be reminded of it as often as possible and in as many ways as possible. If the facilities are not particularly comfortable or attractive, so be it. That is the current situation of the institution and there is no value in burying the fact. In truth, it could help the trustees understand more fully some of the problems faced on a daily basis by the artistic and management leadership of the institution. Regardless of where the meeting is held, every effort should be made not to have the discussions interrupted by telephone calls. Arrangements should be made for messages to be taken and unless there is a real emergency, neither board members nor staff should be called away from the meeting to take a phone call.

The agenda for each meeting of the board of trustees should be prepared in advance and mailed to each member with the reminder notice of the meeting. Initiative for preparing the agenda should be taken by the top management or artistic person in consultation with the board president or chairman. *Any material necessary for a substantive discussion on any topic should be mailed out to board members with the notice of the meeting and the agenda.* For example, if a budget or revised budget is to be discussed, there is absolutely no reason for it not to be sent out with the agenda so that trustees can study it before the meeting. There is nothing worse, nor more disconcerting, than trying to read and absorb a budget seen for the first time, while it is being presented verbally. There is no time for reflective thought and no time to determine if one has any questions about the budget. If there are any changes in figures, since it was mailed out in advance of the meeting, such changes can be introduced at the beginning of the discussion. But this should rarely happen if the staff and the finance committee have done their work properly. The same courtesy should be accorded board members when matters of policy, programs, or new program directions are up for decision.

Board members should prepare themselves for board meetings by reading and studying the material sent to them in advance. It is frustrating for staff and board committee members to find out that trustees have not devoted any time to consideration of materials sent to them.

As indicated earlier in this manual, it is the legal responsibility of board members to be informed and to be prudent. To make decisions on matters of importance to the institution without study, or the opportunity for study, is to act in an uninformed, unwise, and imprudent manner. *Each board should adopt the policy that it will not act on any substantive matter or issue if appropriate information has not been received prior to the meeting where the decision is to be taken.* The only exception to this policy should be in the case of a real emergency or crisis. In such instances, full discussion must be held and board members must feel confident that they are well informed before a vote is taken.

Another aspect of this is the voting by the board on

recommendations made by a board committee. Presumably, the committee has studied the particular matter in depth, assessed the pros and cons of the question, and has come to the board with a recommendation. There is no reason for the full board to go through the same discussions already held by the committee. However, the board members should not feel any inhibition about asking searching questions or seeking more information. Many, however, feel that questioning a committee recommendation in any depth might be considered a delaying action or a questioning of the committee's work. In order to generate productive discussion or to assure the fullest possible understanding of any committee recommendation by all, the committee chairman should highlight for the full board any points of disagreement that may have occurred during the committee discussions and how any such disagreements were resolved. In this way, the committee chairman alerts the board to possible differences of opinion within the committee, or to different interpretations or implications of the recommended action. The board members not serving on that committee then have the opportunity to be more fully informed, thus more rationally responsible for the actions they take through their votes.

All board meetings should have some aspect of fun to them. By fun, it is not meant fun in a party or social sense, but fun in the sense of feeling a part of the creative force of the performing arts institution of which they are trustees. Many times board members who are dedicated to a particular institution become tired or even bored with dealing primarily or sometimes only with fiscal problems and their solutions. Providing a sense of fun usually is the responsibility of the artistic director and his or her staff. *A period of time during each meeting, however limited, should be devoted to discussion related to the very purpose of existence of the institution.* The artistic director's report should not deal primarily with figures about performances but should include the whys of the season artistically, the successes and disappointments of each artistic product, and the whys of this. Also, from time to time, other members of the artistic team (e.g., costume, lighting, and set designers) should be invited to attend board meetings to share their particular artistic expertise with the board. This can result in a much better understanding of the total working and purpose of the institution and can provide a different sense of satisfaction to the board member in terms of the service and reasons for service he or she is giving. *Further, at least one meeting each year should be devoted almost entirely, if not entirely, to a review of where the institution is in terms of its purpose and where it aspires to be.* This might well be one of the meetings resulting from, or as an ongoing part of, the work of an active planning committee. The recapitulation and/or rearticulation of the purpose of the institution gives meaning in depth to the efforts being made by all.

Another suggestion artistic and management leaders as well as board members might consider is to extend an open invitation to all members of the institution to attend board meetings whenever they are free from their work and able to do so. By and large, nothing that goes on in a board meeting is secret or needs to be considered as secret except, as mentioned earlier, specific salary or hiring or firing considerations. As a rule, it should be assumed that if more than one person knows something, it probably will not remain secret for long. Most artistic and management staff of the institution probably will not be able to attend many or any of the meetings, or may not be at all interested in doing so. If the total institution is perceived to be one entity existing and working for the implementation of its artistic purpose, how much better it could be if more of the participants in the institution knew more about each other and the varied responsibilities that make up the whole. It is a question worth serious consideration. It also could help alleviate some of the problems inherent in the we/they syndrome that so often develops.

Chapter 4

Board Retreats

A board retreat provides an opportunity to step back from the day to day operation and problems of the institution in order to look at it as a whole and in the context of what the institution is and wants to be and to then deal with the particular problems or opportunities facing the institution in that context. Board/staff retreats, if properly structured, timed, and facilitated, can be of enormous help to the further development of an institution, if the purpose of holding the retreat is clearly understood. Usually, an individual who is not a board or staff member can facilitate discussion more effectively than can someone closely associated with the organization. *To be productive, a retreat should be facilitated (not led, chaired, or moderated) by someone.*

While the purpose of a board retreat does not need to be articulated in the form of a detailed discussion agenda, there must be a concensus among board members and the artistic and management leadership that the time is right for discussions in depth. Further, there should be a commitment on the part of those participating to attend the retreat from beginning to end.

An example of a valid purpose for a retreat is to provide for an annual review of where the institution has moved and is in terms of its development since the last annual review and to discuss plans for the future. There can be many variations in purpose (e.g., energizing a board, creating the environment for improved board/staff working relationships and understanding), but if the reason for a retreat is not clear to those participating in it, there is less chance of its being successful or ultimately productive.

A retreat is organized to discuss the institution in depth. It should be attended not only by board members, but by at least both the artistic director and managing director. In many instances, more of the staff also might well be included. Staff should not, however, attend the retreat to make presentations. All participants should be in attendance to discuss the institution and its various aspects. Each retreat cannot help but be instructional for all participants, but staff should not overtly attempt to instruct board members through the mechanism of formal presentations. *The environment of the retreat must be one of colleagues working together for and toward a common goal.*

A retreat should not be considered a regular meeting of the board of trustees. During the retreat it is hoped concensus will be reached on a variety of items, but no formal votes or resolutions should be made at the retreat itself. Specific action may be planned, but any formal action necessary to be taken by the board should be voted on at a subsequent regular or special meeting of the board. This provides all participants with the opportunity to reflect on any concensus reached at the retreat before voting, rather than being put into the position of responding to the immediate dynamic of the retreat.

Ideally, a retreat should be held in a comfortable physical environment, removed from the institution or from the site of normal board meetings. The room should be arranged as comfortably and informally as possible. Chalkboards and easels with newsprint and markers should be available. Soft drinks, coffee tea, and juices should be available constantly at the side of the room, not brought in at some predetermined "coffee break" time. Pads and pencils should be provided for each person. Because talking uses up a surprising amount of energy, hard candies should be available to each participant. For the comfort of all, smoking and non-smoking sections of the seating configuration should be established. If at all possible, a telephone should not be in the room.

The scheduled time of the retreat should be clearly stated in advance. It should begin and end at specific times. It is up to the facilitator of the retreat to be sure that meetings start and end on time. Although it is usual that the first session starts somewhat later than scheduled, most individuals respond readily to subsequently being on time if the importance of being on schedule is stressed during the opening remarks. While a great deal can be accomplished within the time frame of one extended day, *it is preferable that a retreat last at least twenty-four hours,* beginning with dinner and a long work session the first evening, starting again immediately after breakfast the following morning and continuing, with a lunch break, until late afternoon. If the institution, or the people participating in the retreat, cannot afford the cost of a twenty-four hour retreat, the discussions can take place during one day. The atmosphere of collegiality and willingness to discuss issues with greater candor seems greater during the course of a twenty-four hour retreat than is the case with the one-day retreat.

There can be great value in having the retreat facilitated by an individual who is not directly associated with the institution. Such a facilitator presumably has no axes to grind vis a vis the institution or the individuals working with and for it and can thus, for example, raise questions and probe issues during the course of the discussion, which an "insider" probably couldn't do in the same way. The outside facilitator also can draw out those who appear reluctant to speak voluntarily and limit somewhat the degree of vocal participation by those who are always willing to comment. While being an outsider, the facilitator should become an integral part of the retreat group if he or she is to be of real assistance. He or she is a facilitator, not a leader or moderator of discussion. In order to be effective, the facilitator needs to know as much as possible about the institution and its structure prior to the start of the retreat. It is most important that the facilitator not presume to have all the answers to the problems of the institution. Rather, he or she should assist the board and staff in their identification of issues and in the evolution and discussion of their options.

While there is no one right way for a retreat to be held, there is a loose adaptable format that can be helpful in terms of discussion of content structure. *First,* all participants should have the opportunity to get to know a little more about each other, particularly in the context of the institution for which they are working collectively. *Second* each participant should be asked to articulate what he or she wants to come out of the retreat. *Third,* time should be spent discussing and articulating the purpose of the institution so that all participants hear from each other at the same time an explanation of the very reason of existence of the institution for which they all are working. It should not be surprising if differences of opinion on purpose arise, but by the end of the discussion of purpose, it is to be hoped there will be a clear concensus. *Fourth,* the discussion should turn to the current programs or activities of the institution and how each of these relates to the purpose. Discussion should include what new programs might be considered to better serve the purpose. *Fifth,* discussion might turn to the question of the people necessary to implement or make possible the programs. This part of the retreat should deal not only with the staff necessary to support the programs but also the role of the board, its present make up of individuals, what gaps exist, its responsibilities, and its best interrelationships of board and staff to provide for a better program implementation, which, in turn, implements purpose. *Sixth,* questions of budget should be dealt with toward the end of the discussion and in the context of the whole. In this way, it can be understood better that budget is a tool to be used in support of programs that are justified because they serve the purpose of the institution. Further, it can be demonstrated that even a limited budget can and should be used to get where the institution wants to go rather than having a perceived limited budget inhibit the institution's development.

The agenda discussed here can serve as a means of getting the discussion of detailed problems or questions into a broader context. Discussion of board membership, structures, and responsibilities, as well as questions pertaining to board/staff relationships can be more meaningful and productive in the context of understanding the whole institution, rather than as isolated topics or problems.

Chapter 5
Sample By-Laws

There is no one set of by-laws that can or should serve as a complete model for all not-for-profit professional performing arts institutions. Each institution should establish its by-laws to provide the structure for its corporate operation in a way that best serves the purpose and implementation of the purpose of the institution. By-laws must not violate any state statutes governing not-for profit corporations. These statutes are easily found, and further assistance or information is available from the group's attorney or such organizations as Volunteer Lawyers for the Arts.

While conforming to the not-for-profit corporation law of the state in which it is incorporated, the institution's by-laws may include provisions not prohibited by law but which might not necessarily be included in the law. For example, the not-for-profit corporation law of a given state may mandate that the corporation be governed by a board of directors. This does not mean that the board of directors provided for in the law may not be called a board of trustees. The term "board of directors" is a direct transfer from the for-profit corporation law into the not-for-profit sector. The term "director" is totally appropriate for a for-profit corporation, but much less so for a not-for-profit one.

The word "trustee" emphasizes the fiduciary responsibility of the "director" of a not-for-profit corporation, a responsibility not emphasized in the directorship of a for-profit corporation. Most private, not-for-profit academic institutions (colleges and universities) are governed by boards of trustees, not by boards of directors, despite the provision in most state not-for-profit corporation laws that such institutions shall be governed by boards of directors. *This is not merely a question of semantics, it is the use of the appropriate title for a governing body having fiduciary responsibility for the institution.*

The following sample set of by-laws should be considered and used as a suggested guideline, a point of departure leading to a final determination of what is best for a particular institution.

By-Laws

of

(corporate name of the institution)

Article I

Name

The name of the corporation is:

Article II

Purpose

The purposes for which this corporation is organized and formed are:
(Note: list statement of purpose)

Article III

Membership

There shall be no members of the Corporation.
(Note: if state law mandates membership, this section should read:
The Board of Trustees shall constitute the membership of the corporation.)

Article IV

Board of Trustees

Section 1. **Purpose, Powers, and Duties.** The Board of Trustees has the general power to 1) control and manage the affairs, funds, and property of the corporation; 2) disburse the Corporation's monies and dispose of its property in fulfillment of its Corporate purpose; provided, however, that the fundamental and basic purposes of the Corporation, as expressed in the Certificate of Incorporation *(Note:* or Articles of Incorporation, or whatever legal title is applied to the instrument of incorporation), shall not thereby be amended or changed, and provided further, that the Board of Trustees shall not permit any part of the net earnings or capital of the Corporation to inure to the benefit of any private individual.

The Board of Trustees shall appoint an Artistic Director and a Managing Director *(Note:* or whatever the appropriate titles are in a particular institution) who shall be responsible to the Board for the artistic, administrative, and business management of the Corporation. The Board of Trustees may further delegate authority to committees or individual Trustees as it deems necessary for the carrying out of the purposes and business of the Corporation. *(Note:* in some institutions, there may be different persons or offices directly appointed by the board. If so, provision should be made here for such appointments.)

Section 2. **Number.** The number of trustees which shall be not less than five (5), shall be fixed from time to time by the Trustees then serving in office, except that a Trustee's term may not be shortened by a reduction in the size of the Board.

Section 3. **Election, Term of Office.** Trustees shall normally be elected at the annual meeting of the Corporation by a majority vote of the Trustees then serving in office. Candidates for board membership shall be nominated for office by a nominating committee. Trustees shall be elected to office for a term of two years (three years), or until their successors are duly elected and qualified, except in the case of their earlier death, resignation, or removal from office. A Trustee may be elected to a second or third consecutive two-year term (second consecutive three-year term), but may not be elected to a fourth consecutive two-year term (third consecutive three-year term). A Trustee may be reelected to the Board after a lapse of one year following completion of three consecutive full two-year terms in office (two consecutive full three-year terms in office). The elected Trustees shall be divided into two classes (three classes) to provide for the election of one-half (one-third) of the elected Trustees at each annual meeting of the Board.

Section 4. **Ex Officio Trustees.** The President (Chairman) of the *(Note:* name of active volunteer support group, e.g., Friends of, Guild of, etc.) shall serve as an ex officio voting member of the Board of Trustees of the Corporation.

From time to time, by majority vote of the Trustees then serving in office, the Board of Trustees may designate additional ex officio Trustees with vote or ex officio Trustees without vote. Ex officio Trustees with vote shall be counted in determining whether or not a quorum is present at a meeting. Ex officio Trustees without vote shall not be counted in determining the presence of a quorum. *(Note:* inherent in this section is the ability of the Board to accord ex officio Trustee status, with or without vote, to the Artistic Director and/or Managing Director.)

Section 5. **Resignation and Removal of Trustees.** Any Trustee may resign by giving written notice of his or her resignation to the Board or to the President or Secretary of the Corporation. Such resignation shall take effect at the time specified in such notice and the acceptance of such resignation shall not be necessary to make it effective. Any trustee may be removed, with or without cause, by a two-thirds vote of all Trustees then serving in office.

Section 6. **Vacancies.** Vacancies in the Board, however arising, shall be filled by a majority vote of all Trustees then serving in office at any regular meeting of the Board or at a special meeting of the Board called for that purpose. Persons shall be nominated for Trusteeship by the Nominating Committee and the list of any such nominees shall be included with the notice of the meeting at which election is proposed.

Article V

Meetings

Section 1. **Annual Meeting.** The annual meeting of the Corporation shall be held during the month of (name of month) each year, or on such other date as may be fixed by the Board of Trustees.

Section 2. **Regular Meeting.** The frequency and dates of regular meetings of the Board of Trustees shall be fixed by the Board of

Trustees, normally at its annual meeting.

Section 3. **Special Meetings.** Special meetings of the Board of Trustees may be called by the President or Vice President of the Board or shall be called at the request of any three voting Trustees of the Board.

Section 4. **Place of Meetings.** Meetings of the Board may be held at the principal offices of the Corporation or at any other place within or without the State of (name of State). The notice of the meeting shall include the place and time of the meeting.

Section 5. **Notice of Meetings.** Written notice of the time and place of the annual and regular meetings shall be sent to each Trustee to the last known place of business or residence of the Trustee at least ten days, but not more than thirty days, prior to the date of such meetings. Written notice of special meetings shall be sent to each Trustee to the last known place of business or residence of each Trustee not less than four days prior to the date of such meeting or by telegraph or telephone not less than two days prior to the date of such meeting.

Section 6. **Waiver.** Notwithstanding the provisions of any of the foregoing sections, a meeting of the Board of Trustees may be held at such time or place within or without the State of (name of State) as the Board of Trustees shall designate and any action may be taken thereat, if notice thereof is waived in writing by every Trustee having the right to vote at the meeting.

Section 7. **Quorum.** Unless provided for differently elsewhere in these By-Laws, a majority of the Trustees then serving in office shall constitute a quorum for all meetings of the Board of Trustees. *(Note: each institution should determine its quorum very carefully.)*

In the absence of a quorum, a majority of the Trustees present may, without giving notice other than announcement at the meeting, adjourn the meeting from time to time until a quorum is obtained. At any such adjourned meeting at which a quorum is present, any business may be transacted which might have been transacted at the meeting as originally called.

Section 8. **Voting.** At any meeting of the Trustees, every voting Trustee present in person at such meeting shall be entitled to one vote and, except as otherwise provided by law or by these By-Laws, the act of a majority of the Trustees present in person at any meeting at which a quorum is present shall be the act of the Trustees.

Article VI

Officers

Section 1. **Principal Officers.** The principal officers of the Corporation shall be a President, a Vice President, a Treasurer, and a Secretary. The President, Vice President, and Treasurer shall be elected from among the Trustees then serving in office. The Board of Trustees at any meeting may by resolution elect or appoint additional officers or engage agents and employees and determine their terms of office and compensation, if any, as it may deem advisable. *(Note:* this section provides that the Secretary may or may not be a Trustee).

Section 2. **Election and Term of Office.** The officers of the Corporation shall normally be elected at the annual meeting of the Board of Trustees, but may be elected at any meeting of the Board at which a quorum is present, by a vote of the majority of the Trustees present in person at the meeting. The Nominating Committee shall prepare a list of nominations for officer positions and such list shall be mailed to each Trustee then serving, along with the notice of said meeting. An officer shall be elected to serve a one-year term and shall hold office until the next annual meeting of the Board following election or until his or her successor shall have been elected, except in the case of death, resignation, or removal as provided for in these By-Laws. No Trustee may serve in one office for more than three consecutive one-year terms. Tenure for the office of Secretary is not limited.

Section 3. **Removal of Officers.** Any officer may be removed, with or without cause, at any time at any Board meeting at which a quorum is present by a vote of two-thirds of the Trustees then serving in office.

Section 4. **Vacancies.** Vacancies among the officers, however arising, shall be filled by a majority vote of Trustees present at any regular or special meeting of the Board at which there is a quorum present. The list of nominations for officer positions shall be included with the notice of the meeting at which election is proposed.

Section 5. **President.** The President shall preside at all meetings of the Board and generally do and perform all acts incident to the office of President, and shall have such additional powers and duties as may from time to time be assigned to him or her by the Board. Unless otherwise provided for in these By-Laws, the President shall be an ex officio voting member of each Board committee.

Section 6. **Vice President.** In the absence (or inability to act) of the President, the Vice President shall exercise the powers and perform the duties of President. The Vice President shall also generally assist the President and shall have such other powers and perform such other duties as may from time to time be designated by the President or by the Board.

Section 7. **Treasurer.** The Treasurer shall act under the supervision of the Board and shall have charge and custody of, and be responsible for, all the funds of the Corporation and shall keep or cause to be kept, and shall be responsible for the keeping of, accurate and adequate records of the assets, liabilities, and transactions of the Corporation. He or she shall deposit, or cause to be deposited, all monies and other valuable effects of the Corporation in the name of and to the credit of the Corporation in such banks, trust companies, or other depositories as may be designated from time to time by the Board. He or she shall disburse, or cause to be disbursed, the funds of the Corporation based upon proper vouchers for such disbursement. In general, he or she shall perform all the duties incident to the office of Treasurer and such other duties as may from time to time be assigned to him or her by the President or the Board.

Section 8. **Secretary.** The Secretary shall act as Secretary of, and keep the minutes of all meetings of, the Board in one or more books provided for that purpose and shall see that minutes of meetings of the Board are distributed promptly to all members of the Board. He or she shall see that all notices are duly given in accordance with these By-Laws and as required by law. He or she shall be custodian of the seal of the Corporation and shall affix and attest the seal to any and all documents the execution of which on behalf of the Corporation under its seal shall have been specifically or generally authorized by the Board. He or she shall have charge of the books, records, and papers of the Corporation relating to its organization as a corporation and shall see that all reports, statements, and other documents required by law are properly kept or filed, except to the extent that the same are to be kept or filed by the Treasurer. In general, he or she shall perform all the duties incident to the office of Secretary and such other duties as may from time to time be assigned to him or her by the President or by the Board.

Section 9. **Bonding.** Any officer or employee of the Corporation shall, if required by the Board of Trustees, give such security for the faithful performance of his or her duties as the Board of Trustees may require.

Article VII

Committees

Section 1. The Board may by resolution at any meeting of the Board designate standing and/or ad hoc committees of the Board.

Section 2. **Membership.** Each standing committee shall consist of at least three members, at least one of whom shall be a member of the Board. Unless otherwise provided for in these By-Laws or by the laws of the State of (name of State), the chairman of each standing and ad hoc committee shall be appointed by the President of the Board.

Unless otherwise provided for in the these By-Laws, any standing or ad hoc committee designated by the Board of Trustees may include as full voting members of such committees such persons, whether or not Trustees or Officers of the Corporation, as the Board of Trustees shall determine. Each such committee shall have power to the extent delegated to it by the Board and in accordance with the laws of the State of (name of State). Each committee shall keep minutes of proceedings and report to the Board of Trustees. At least one member of the artistic or management staff of the Corporation shall be an ex officio member *(Note:* with or without vote) of each committee.

Section 3. **Standing Committees.** The following standing committees shall be established by the Board of Trustees: Executive Committee, Nominating Committee, Finance Committee, Fund Raising Committee, Planning Committee. *(Note:* the Planning Committee may be further defined, e.g., Long-Range Planning Committee, Strategic Planning Committee.)

a.) *Executive Committee.* The Executive Committee shall include in its membership the officers of the Corporation and the chairman of the standing committees. Unless a different person is designated Chairman of the Executive Committee by resolution of the Board, the President of the Board shall serve as Chairman. All members of the Executive Committee shall be voting members of the Board of Trustees.

The Executive Committee shall, during intervals between meetings of the Board, exercise all the powers of the Board in the management of the business and affairs of the Corporation, except as otherwise provided by law, these By-Laws, or by resolution of the Board. The presence of a majority of the members of the Executive Committee then serving in office shall be necessary and sufficient to constitute a quorum and the act of a majority of the members of the Executive Committee present at a meeting of the Committee at which a quorum is present, shall be the act of the Committee. The Committee shall keep full and fair records and accounts of its proceedings and transactions. The minutes of the Executive Committee shall be distributed to all members of the Board of Trustees. All actions by the Committee shall be reported to the Board at its next meeting and shall be subject to approval by the Board.

b.) *Nominating Committee.* The Nominating Committee shall review regularly the needs of the Corporation in regard to Board membership and shall propose a slate of nominees for election as Trustees at each annual meeting of the Board or at any other meeting of the Board at which Trustees will be elected. The Nominating Committee also shall propose a slate of Officers of the Corporation for election at each annual meeting of the Board. The Nominating Committee also shall nominate Trustees and/or Officers to fill vacancies occurring for whatever reason, as provided for in Article IV, section 6 and in Article VI, section 4 of these

By-Laws. The designation of Chairman and members of the Nominating Committee shall be approved by resolution of the Board at the annual meeting of the Board of Trustees. The Chairman and members of the Nominating Committee shall not serve on this committee for more than three consecutive one-year terms. The President of the Board of Trustees shall not serve as a member of the Nominating Committee. *(Note:* See Article VI, section 5.)

c.) *Finance Committee.* The Finance Committee shall work with the staff of the Corporation in the preparation of an annual budget, shall review the finances of the Corporation on a regular basis, and shall make recommendations to the Board of Trustees. The Treasurer of the Corporation shall serve as a voting member of the Finance Committee.

d.) *Fund Raising Committee.* The Fund Raising Committee is responsible for and shall assist the staff in planning for and implementing plans for the acquisition of all contributed income necessary to the financial stability of the Corporation.

e.) *Planning Committee.* The Planning Committee shall be concerned actively with matters involving the future development of programs as well as systems and structures to implement the artistic purposes of the Corporation.

Section 4. **Committee Meetings.** Unless otherwise provided for in these By-Laws, a majority of the members then serving on a Committee constitutes a quorum for the meeting of the Committee and the vote of a simple majority of those present at a meeting at which a quorum is present, constitutes an action of the Committee. Each Committee shall determine and schedule the number of regular meetings it will hold each year.

Article VIII

Indemnification

Every person who is or shall be or shall have been a Trustee or Officer of the Corporation and his or her personal representatives shall be idemnified by the Corporation against all costs and expenses reasonably incurred by or imposed upon him or her in connection with or resulting from any action, suit, or proceeding to which he or she may be made a party by reason of his or her being or having been a Trustee or Officer of the Corporation or of any subsidiary or affiliate thereof, except in relation to such matters as to which he or she shall finally be adjudicated in such action, suit, or proceeding to have acted in bad faith and to have been liable by reason of willful misconduct or willful negligence in the performance of his or her duty as Trustee or Officer. Costs and expenses of actions for which this Article provides indemnification shall include, among other things, attorneys' fees, damages, and reasonable amounts paid in settlement. (*Note:* there may be different State laws regarding indemnification which could affect the working of the indemnification article. Also the article has little practical meaning unless the Corporation carries indemnification insurance.)

Article IX

Miscellaneous

Section 1. **Fiscal Year.** The fiscal year of the Corporation shall be (specify beginning and ending dates).

Section 2. **Contracts, Checks, Bank Accounts, Etc.** The Board of Trustees is authorized to select such banks or depositories as it shall deem proper for the funds of the Corporation. The Board shall determine who, if anyone, in addition to the President and the Treasurer, shall be authorized from time to time on the Corporation's behalf to sign checks, drafts, or other orders for the payment of money, acceptances, notes, or other evidences of indebtedness, to enter into contracts or to execute and deliver other documents and instruments.

Section 3. **Corporate Seal.** (*Note:* if one is required by law or one is desired.) The seal of the Corporation shall be circular in form and shall bear the name of the Corporation, the name of the State, and the year of incorporation.

Article X

Amendments

These By-Laws may be altered, amended, or repealed in whole or in part at any duly organized meeting of the Board of Trustees of the Corporation, by a two-thirds majority vote of the Trustees then serving in office. Any proposal to amend these By-Laws shall be included with the notice of the meeting at which the amendment is proposed.